Twomey

MW01008008

Passionate Slugs
& Hollywood Frogs

Passionate Slugs & Hollywood Frogs

An Uncommon Field Guide
to Northwest Backyards

Patricia K. Lichen
Illustrated by Linda M. Feltner

SASQUATCH BOOKS
SEATTLE

Copyright ©2001 by Patricia K. Lichen
Illustrations copyright ©2001 by Linda M. Feltner
All rights reserved. No portion of this book may be reproduced or utilized in any form, or by any electronic, mechanical, or other means without the prior written permission of the publisher.

Printed in Canada
Distributed in Canada by Raincoast Books, Ltd.
07 06 05 04 03 02 01   6 5 4 3 2 1

Cover and interior design and composition: Kate Basart
Copy editor: Alice Copp Smith

Library of Congress Cataloging in Publication Data
Passionate slugs and Hollywood frogs : an uncommon field guide to Northwest backyards / by Patricia Lichen ; illustrations by Linda Feltner.
        p. cm.
        References; index.
        1. Natural history—Northwest, Pacific. 2. Urban animals—Northwest, Pacific—Identification. 3. Urban plants—Northwest, Pacific—Identification. I. Title
QH104.5.N6 L29 2001
508.795—dc21   00-052264

Sasquatch Books
615 Second Avenue
Seattle, Washington 98104
(206) 467-4300
www.SasquatchBooks.com
books@SasquatchBooks.com

To my Mom, Mae Rue Hutchison,
for the Girl Scout hikes and campouts she endured,

and my Dad, Frederick J. Hutchison,
for watching Jacques Cousteau *and* Wild Kingdom *with me.*

And to my daughter, Hallie Rose Lichen,
friend of earthworms, daddy longlegs, and pillbugs.
May you never outgrow the connection.

Contents

Acknowledgments

I am grateful to the following experts, each of whom graciously reviewed at least one (and more often several) of these essays: Ric Balfour of the Oregon Forest Resources Institute; Sandra Diedrich; Sarah Gage of the University of Washington Herbarium; John Meriwether; Jim McIver; Susan Piper; Robert Michael Pyle; Shelley Weisberg of the North Cascades Institute; and Matt Zaffino, KGW-TV chief meteorologist. They pointed out errors and misinterpretations wherever these reared their ugly heads. Any inaccuracies that remain in these essays are mine alone.

My thanks also to these friends and family members who have shared with me encounters with the natural world, and then allowed me to tell those stories: my sister-in-law Treesa Beaton; Esther Howard; my mother, Mae Rue Hutchison; Hallie and Tim Lichen; Jim McIver (who also supplied information about the western thatching ants); Ralph Naess; Torgy Torgersen; and Jenni Whitney.

I am also indebted to my father, Frederick J. Hutchison, and the members of two writers' groups, Sirius Writers and Chrysalis, who critiqued and improved many of these essays. Special thanks to the stalwart Susan McElheran who, in belonging to both groups, critiqued more of these essays than anyone short of my editor. Among the Sirius Writers, I especially thank Bonnie and Gale Long, Jim Manuel, Dwight Ball Morrill, Tawny Schlieski, and Cord "Bud" Sengstake. Among the Chrysalis group at Clackamas Community College in Oregon City, Oregon, I especially thank Beth Miles, who critiqued many essays outside of the meetings, and our leader, Kate Gray (a woman with altitude). I am also grateful to the members of both groups for their unstinting encouragement and enthusiasm for this project.

Introduction

"The birds I heard today, which fortunately, did not come within the scope of my science, sang as freshly as if it had been the first morning of creation." I've always loved this quote by Henry David Thoreau, which reminds me that I don't need to know the name of a songbird (or a fern or a mushroom or a hawk, for that matter) to enjoy it.

Yet, as Thoreau certainly knew, there is joy in being able to recognize a plant or creature wherever we find it, and to greet it by name. As with our other friendships, the more we learn about a particular being's life, the greater our appreciation can grow.

This is the purpose of the *Uncommon Field Guide* series: to enhance our connection to other beings in the natural world, and hopefully to deepen that connection. Each of the three books (*Passionate Slugs & Hollywood Frogs: An Uncommon Field Guide to Northwest Backyards; Brittle Stars & Mudbugs: An Uncommon Field Guide to Northwest Shorelines & Wetlands;* and *River-Walking Songbirds & Singing Coyotes: An Uncommon Field Guide to Northwest Mountains*) offers an opportunity to become better acquainted with plants, animals, and phenomena (such as rainbows or lightning) found in the Pacific Northwest.

In each book I've focused on easily recognizable species and phenomena, and those common to a particular Pacific Northwest geographic area. Of course, some of the subjects do not neatly segregate themselves into specific territories, and for that reason their placement has been arbitrary. (For example, the crow, coyote, and horsetails might have ended up in any one of the three books—but the crows landed in the backyard book, coyote found a home in the mountain book, and horsetails sprouted in the shorelines and wetlands book.)

With apologies to those of you living in the eastern part of Washington and Oregon, the essays in all three books focus to a greater degree on the region west of the Cascade Mountains. Please note I often use the shortcut of "Pacific Northwest region" instead of the more accurate (but too cumbersome) phrase "Pacific Northwest region west of the Cascades."

For many years I had the pleasure of working as a naturalist in Washington and Oregon, discussing with people the plants, animals, and natural events of the Pacific Northwest as we walked through woods and beside waterfalls, down into caves and along lakeshores. It's my hope that the *Uncommon Field Guide* series continues that work, acting in the capacity of a friendly naturalist who answers your questions, mentions interesting tidbits you might not think to ask, and helps to further both your understanding and your relationship with the natural world.

Attracting Wildlife to Your Backyard

You can become a wildlife manager in your own backyard. No matter what size your yard might be (and even if it's only a city apartment balcony), you can make changes that will draw in animals.

You don't need a degree in biology or wildlife management to create a haven for birds, butterflies, and small mammals. You just need to supply what they are searching for: water, food, shelter, and places to rear their young.

One of the easiest and fastest ways to attract wildlife is to provide a year-round water supply. Despite the Northwest's notorious propensity toward rain, our summer months can be quite dry, and winter's puddles occasionally freeze over. Water—offered in something as simple as a plastic plant saucer or as ambitious as a new backyard pond—is a powerful attractant. Animals in need of a drink, a bath, a swimming hole, or a place to lay eggs will seek it out.

Many people already provide food for birds, at least in winter. If you've found that the birds seem to scatter more of the feed than they ingest, it's probably the fault of your seed choice rather than the sloppy habits of your guests. Some mostly-millet seed mixes (such as the plastic-bagged type typically sold in grocery stores) are produced in the East and Midwest, so they contain the type of food that bird species found there appreciate. Our Western birds are better served by feed from local wild-bird stores, feed stores, or other outlets. Black oil sunflower seeds are a general crowd-pleaser; additional choices at the buffet (such as Niger thistle, cracked corn, or fruit) will attract specific types of birds such as finches, mourning doves, or cedar waxwings. And, of course, hummingbirds dote on sugar water (but don't add any red dye—it's unnecessary, and possibly harmful).

Such offerings are a wonderful bonus for the birds that visit your yard. But an easy way to attract a wide range of bird species, as well as other

animals, is to include native plants in your yard. After all, native plants co-evolved with the native animals and once covered your homesite before it was converted to human habitat. Planting natives helps retain the Northwest's natural plant diversity; they also require less maintenance and watering, and they look lovely to boot. Some native shrubs particularly attractive to wildlife are salal, Indian plum, evergreen huckleberry, snowberry, vine maple, red osier dogwood, Oregon grape, red elderberry, thimbleberry, salmonberry, and red-flowering currant.

Native plants also create excellent cover (shelter from the weather as well as from enemies—including neighborhood cats). Vegetation of various heights and types, including trees, bushes, and vines, will offer different hiding options, as will a rock wall, a brush pile, a log, or a dead tree left standing. These places can also become nurseries that help maintain the population of wildlife. Adding bird, bat, native mason bee, and butterfly boxes to your yard also encourages these animals.

The needs of wildlife for water, food, shelter, and nesting areas are quite understandable, but it may seem a bit daunting to figure out the best way to supply these things. Happily, there are many organizations, Internet sites, workshops, books, and other publications available to help people create wildlife-friendly habitats.

The National Wildlife Federation has been guiding people in the creation of "backyard habitats" since 1973. More recently, it has extended its program to specifically include schoolyards and workplaces and to encourage "citizen naturalists" to share their knowledge. You can contact local offices in larger cities such as Portland and Seattle, or follow the advice found in the Federation's book *Gardening for Wildlife* or on its web site, www.nwf.org/habitats.

The Washington Department of Fish and Wildlife offers a series of handouts under the title "Urban Wildlife Series" as well as a book entitled *Landscaping for Wildlife in the Pacific Northwest,* and the Oregon Department of Fish and Wildlife publishes the book *Naturescaping: A Place for Wildlife.* City programs such as Portland's Naturescaping for Clean Rivers offer workshops and other events.

Black-Capped Chickadee

Latin name: Parus *atricapillus*

Description: 4½ inches; small, plump bird with black bib and cap; white cheeks.

Habitat: Open woodlands, especially deciduous, but also those mixed with conifers; clearings; suburbs.

Chickadees remind me of Boy Scouts. They seem cheerful, brave, and even thrifty in the way they select one seed at a time. Chickadees are energetic visitors to outdoor feeders, zipping in to nab a sunflower seed and zooming right off. If you keep a close eye on one, you may see it flit to a nearby branch, brace the seed against its perch and pry out the meat inside, or cache the seed for a later day.

The busy little birds aren't picky eaters. In addition to everything offered at the feeder—peanuts, seeds, or suet—they'll consume flies, wasps, caterpillars, ants, aphids, and other insects, as well as snails, conifer seeds, berries, and other wild fruit. They're acrobatic when feeding, hanging upside down or sideways on a tree as readily as they perch right side up.

Chickadees are gregarious birds until their mating season in spring, when they pair off. They are hole-nesters, but their blunt beaks limit the kinds of trees they can call home; they prefer one that is well-rotted or a softwood tree such as birch. When they excavate a hole, they'll carry the wood chips some distance away to avoid alerting predators. They'll also nest in old woodpecker holes, gourds, and birdhouses. If you set up a birdhouse for them, scatter sawdust or wood chips inside so they can do a bit of excavating.

Inside the hole, the female builds a cushiony nest from moss, feathers, and bits of fur, hair, wool, or insect cocoons. She lays an egg a day for six to eight days while the male finds food and brings it to her. If the female is harassed while sitting on the nest, she'll defend her young with a surprising explosive hiss that sounds like a snake. She stays on the eggs for nearly two weeks. If she leaves for a few minutes, which is rare, she'll first cover the eggs with part of their warm cushion.

When the young hatch, it takes a concerted effort by both parents to feed the six to eight hungry chicks. The parents make two hundred and fifty or more daily trips to the nest with food. Their greedy young gobble down the caterpillars and insect larvae and yell for more. More than three hectic weeks after hatching, the young are ready to leave the nest and follow their parents around, learning how to forage and take care of themselves. Once they are fully grown, they disperse to find their own territories.

Chickadees are frequent visitors to backyard bird feeders, and because

they are among the tamest of birds, you can sometimes get quite close to them. One winter's day I was in a hurry to run a errand when I noticed the feeder was low on sunflower seeds. I usually wait for a lull in the action to refill it, but I decided to interrupt the feeding birds rather than let the feeder run out while I was gone. The birds scattered at my approach, landing in various nearby trees. To my surprise, chickadees and nuthatches landed beside me in the very tree the feeder hung from. Inspired by their trust, I scooped up a heaping handful and offered it to them. In a few minutes they were eating out of my gloved hand, their feathered weight so slight that only my eyes told me they were really there.

If you want to hand-feed a wild bird, chickadees are among the best to approach because they are so curious and trusting. It may take several tries to convince a bird to approach, but when one of these little charmers feeds regularly from your hand, you can add "loyal" to their list of Scout-like qualities.

Common Raccoon

Latin name: *Procyon lotor*

Description: To 35 inches long, including 12-inch tail; pointed face with black "bandit mask"; body thick-set and grizzled gray; bushy tail ringed alternating gray and black.

Habitat: From the coast to mid-elevations in the mountains; urban, suburban, or rural areas; frequently near fresh or salt water.

When opportunity knocks, raccoons open the door. A chimney, a tree, or a storm drain will serve as a place to spend the daylight hours; seafood, meat, garden vegetables, or pet food left out on a porch are all delectable food items. The raccoon's den, and its dinner, are largely determined by whatever it finds in front of its little black nose. And the animal's ability to walk, swim, and climb allows it to exploit any number of situations. Unlike many other species, the opportunistic raccoon is doing as well today as it was before Europeans arrived to transform the continent.

Their capable little "hands" are another reason these mammals fare so well. The five fingers on each forefoot can feel around for unseen food in mud or water, capture moving prey, and reach into promising crevices and hollows. Raccoons can open cupboard doors and garbage cans. And it's well known that they use those forefeet to "wash" their food, although this activity has mainly been seen in captive animals—and "dunking" is probably a more appropriate description. Various interesting, but disproven, theories have been advanced to explain the behavior. It was once thought that the animals needed to soften their food before consuming it, or had underdeveloped salivary glands. Some biologists currently speculate that, since many of their natural foods are found in muddy water (including a favorite, crayfish), the behavior may have evolved as a way to rid the food of some mud and debris. In any case, raccoons also readily dine away from water.

These animals prowl about looking for food during the late evening and nighttime hours, all year round. Although they fatten up for the winter, raccoons don't hibernate. Each has a number of dens in its territory and, like a true bandit, tends to spend only one day in any particular place before moving on to the next. A den might be a hollow in a tree, or a hole under its roots, or another animal's underground burrow. Rock crevices can be suitable, or the spaces under porches or in culverts. A raccoon's bed only has to be big enough for one, unless it's breeding or child-rearing time.

The mostly solitary animals may spend a night or two together during mating time, and then the hopeful male leaves to seek other females. After a gestation of around two months, the female births two to four babies, each about four inches long. Although they are relatively sparsely haired, the marks of facial mask and ringed tail are already evident on their skin. At first, the mother leaves her babies alone for only short periods of time as she forages near the den. As the youngsters grow, she wanders farther afield, for longer periods of time, and eventually the young begin to follow her on nocturnal ramblings. As autumn approaches, they stay on their mother's territory but become more independent. During the cold months, they may still bed down with her or with siblings.

Great horned owls and bobcats may prey on raccoons, but humans take by far the greatest number. Raccoons are killed as nuisances, hunted for sport, and trapped for fur. Their fur was especially favored in the 1920s by college men, who wore long raccoon coats, and by boys in the 1960s who, inspired by the *Daniel Boone* television show, wore coonskin caps with dangling tails.

Despite fashion crazes, modern life has not appreciably impeded the versatile raccoons. In addition to catholic palates and habitats, the animals' humanlike forepaws help them to adapt to a modern environment. Raccoons are equally prepared to forage for wild food in the forest or to dumpster-dive in the city.

Eastern Gray Squirrel

Latin name: *Sciurus carolinensis*

Description: 18 inches long including 9-inch tail; grizzled gray hairs on upper body, light-gray to white belly; may also be all black.

Habitat: Suburban yards and urban parks and gardens.

If you spot a gray-colored squirrel in an urban yard or in a city park, it's more likely to be an introduced eastern gray, or perhaps the larger and more reddish eastern fox squirrel, than one of our native western grays. The smaller western gray squirrel prefers oak woodlands and tends to avoid people. (Douglas squirrels are also smaller and shyer, but their coats are brownish, with orange undersides.) The more aggressive immigrants are happy to accept—or demand—a handout from people.

Both eastern gray and eastern fox squirrels were purposely released in Western cities, on campuses and on large private estates. Gray squirrels were introduced to Seattle in 1925 and to Stanley Park in Vancouver, B.C., in 1914 (some of the latter are black rather than gray).

Wherever they make their homes, squirrels have specific territories that meet their requirements for food and shelter, and these territories overlap. Local squirrels recognize each other by sight and smell, and establish a dominance hierarchy: generally, older squirrels have dominance over younger, and male over female. The ranking allows them to live peaceably (most of the time) within their overlapping territories.

Eastern gray squirrel "mating chases" usually occur twice a year, December to February and June to July. A receptive female climbs high into the treetops and broadcasts a personals ad. She repeats a specific call (which has been described as "ducklike") to attract males from neighboring territories and beyond. Interested males respond by dropping what they're doing and rushing to meet her. She leads her admirers (from two to a dozen) on a frantic, noisy chase around and among the trees. It's speculated that the chase induces the female to ovulate. It also helps the suitors determine dominance and decides who will mate with her.

About forty-four days later, three to five helpless and hairless young are born in a tree cavity nest that the female vigorously defends. The mother nurses her young for several weeks but does not bring them food. At about six or seven weeks, the young squirrels make their first tentative forays outside the nest, where they discover tasty insects and tender buds. At ten to twelve weeks, the young are weaned and on their own, and their mother is preparing for another brood.

Squirrels eat seeds, fruit, insects, bird eggs, corn, mushrooms (including the deadly amanita), and, of course, nuts. When the supply of nuts exceeds the squirrels' eating capacity, the animals begin caching. Studies suggest that squirrels don't really remember where they buried each nut. Instead, they depend on random searches of areas that seem like prime places to bury nuts. When they get close, their sense of smell helps them home in on an individual nut; squirrels can smell a nut buried under several inches of soil or snow.

People who feed birds sometimes find that squirrels are liable to help themselves to the offerings. Some bird lovers find this annoying or even rude (as if the squirrels ought to realize the food is there for *birds*). But there are books that suggest ways to outwit squirrels, and some people enjoy creating obstacles that the ingenious squirrels must surmount in order to earn their sunflower seeds. Other people plagued by squirrels have simply decided to give up and enjoy watching their antics. Offering corn or nuts in an area some distance away from the bird feeder can help satisfy the squirrels and preserve the seeds.

Like birds, squirrels can build nests. Although they prefer to nest in old woodpecker holes in winter and when raising young, during summer they build round nests of leaves and branches. These are situated close to the trees' trunks and are often visible during the autumn and winter months. Eastern gray squirrels spend their nights safely tucked into their homes. They greet the new day bright-eyed and bushy-tailed, ready to accept food from humans—be it a free handout or stolen goods.

Deer Mouse

Latin name: *Peromyscus maniculatus*
Description: Body 3 to 4 inches long and 2- to 5-inch tail; brown or gray above, white underparts.
Habitat: Virtually everywhere except open water and in dense city centers.

One of my fellow naturalists at Mount St. Helens National Volcanic Monument liked to test the gullibility of tourists by claiming that deer mice had little antlers. Ralph maintained that during the rutting season the forests rang with the clashes of the males. Eventually he would have to confess that the (antlerless) mice might have gotten their common name simply because their coloration is similar to that of deer. Even their tails are two-toned: tawny above and white below. (This is one way to differentiate them from the introduced Eurasian house mouse, which is more likely to inhabit city dwellings.)

Deer mice are so abundant and accommodating in their choice of habitats that they could be found everywhere around the volcanic monument: in the ancient lava tubes, the clearcuts, the old-growth forests, the ash-covered eruption zone—and in the Forest Service bunkhouses. When I moved in for the summer, I found I had dozens of four-footed roommates. My human housemates and I quickly learned to pack all our food into sturdy, airtight plastic containers and to ignore nocturnal rustlings. It was harder to ignore being awakened in the night by tiny feet running across my chest— and impossible to overlook the mother and five pink babies I found nestled in my underwear drawer one morning.

Deer mice make their homes just about anywhere. Males and females alike make nests in logs, burrows, trees, shrubbery, empty bird's nests, and other cozy places, where they sleep away the daylight hours. These nests grow foul after a month or so, and the mouse moves on, although it may return after the nest has had a good airing out. Nests are made of whatever is handy: mosses, cattail seeds, string, shredded insulation—or underwear.

Deer mice get busy shortly before sunrise, scampering out of their nests in a furtive quest for food. Their diet includes seeds, nuts, grains, caterpillars, crickets, grasshoppers, beetles—or whatever they find in a kitchen's cupboards. Throughout the year, but especially in the fall, mice cache food supplies for later lean times.

Because they are found nearly everywhere and are timid little creatures with no defenses, deer mice are a staple in the diet of nearly every carnivorous animal. The deer mouse's survival strategy is simple: outbreed all the predators. Accordingly, they achieve sexual maturity at only two months of age and have three to five young after a short gestation of twenty-three days, which allows two to four litters a year. A new mother may go into estrus a day or two after giving birth. If she is impregnated while still nursing, the egg will have a delayed implantation. Still, she will have to leave her weaned young in the first nest to give birth in a second nest. The older offspring stay in their nest a while longer before leaving to seek their fortunes.

The newborn babies I found that morning in my drawer were obviously not leaving anytime soon. I enlisted the help of a fellow naturalist, who nabbed the docile mother by the base of the tail while I scooped up her babies. We carried them to a crevice outside that I had already lined with nesting material. But when I checked a few hours later, I wasn't surprised to find that the mother had carried her young to some location she deemed more suitable.

After that, I launched a benign war against the little creatures. Reluctant to nail them with conventional traps, I bought a Havahart trap and began live-trapping them. The sound of the little door slamming shut woke us three or four times a night until we got used to it. I released all the captives into the meadows and woods, knowing that to a deer mouse practically any habitat would be as acceptable—if not as desirable—as the Forest Service bunkhouse.

Townsend's Mole

Latin name: *Scapanus townsendii*

Description: To 9 inches, including 1½-inch tail; dark fur; tiny eyes and ears; tapering snout; broad, pale forepaws; pink tail more or less hairless.

Habitat: Lawns, pastures, meadows, fields, golf courses.

You already know why mole tunnels are considered bad: those unsightly dirt mounds and annoying ridges mar an otherwise smooth lawn. But here are a few reasons mole tunnels might be considered good. Their digging churns mineral-rich subsoil up where plant roots can access it; the tunnels provide drainage for excess water; and the tunnels also aerate the soil, thereby improving plant growth and preventing erosion. But try convincing an irate farmer, homeowner, or golf course manager that those ridges are beneficial.

Okay, a mole may not exactly be a superhero, but its muscular upper torso make it look somewhat like one. If you knew nothing about the lifestyles of moles, their hefty shoulders, and especially those long-clawed, amazingly meaty "hands," would give you a clue to their subterranean powers. Additional adaptations to the below-ground life include minute eyes (vision is not very important in the dark), sensitive ears and snout that register vibrations, and a narrow pelvis that allows moles to turn easily— even somersault to change direction—in their narrow tunnels. Because their fur, like velvet, has no nap, the hair can be comfortably pressed in any direction. This allows moles to travel forward or backward in their tight tunnels without being rubbed the wrong way.

Moles like their solitude; the only time they purposely come together is to mate. This occurs early in the year, and the male apparently seeks the female in her burrow. Once this duty is dispensed with, the parents-to-be go their separate ways. Shortly before her young are born, the female digs a nursery chamber, often located near or directly underneath a noticeably large mound of aboveground dirt called the "fortress." The mother also constructs a nest, usually of grass. The inner layer is comprised of dry grasses, while the outer layer has green, wet grasses which, as they decompose, will help heat the nest. When her preparations are complete, the mother births two or three young. These remain with her for a little over a month. When the young disperse they make a perilous overland journey under cover of darkness. Most find a suitable place to dig in within thirty yards of their natal chamber. Like their parents, they now begin creating an elaborate system of tunnels.

Moles make two kinds of tunnels. The first type, a shallow tunnel used only one time for foraging, is marked by sinuous humped ridges that show where the mole hunted, pushing up the soil with its back. Earthworms are a mole's favorite prey, but the omnivorous creatures also dig centipedes, ants, snails, slugs, various kinds of insect larvae, and pasture grasses. (Your garden plants don't generally interest them; if these are being attacked from below ground, the more likely culprits are gophers or voles.) The best way for a homeowner to deal with the ridges is to simply press them back down and perhaps water them to seal the deal.

Molehills mark the second kind of tunnel—the one that's usually more of a problem to the homeowner. When digging its deeper travelways, which it will use often, the mole has to get rid of the excess soil somehow. If the soil is loose, the animal may simply compact it as it digs, and no molehills will appear. But soil already compacted will require excavation to the surface—and that means molehills. These are not entrances or exits, but simply dome-shaped mounds of mole mine tailings. The dirt piles are usually about six or eight inches high, but molehills can seem like mountains when you run a lawn mower over one. Spreading out the pile with a little digging of your own will smooth out the problem.

If you want to rid your lawn of moles, there are any number of traps you can buy or home remedies you can attempt. These range from sinking empty bottles into the tunnels so that the necks stick out at an angle to the wind (the resulting piping is said to drive off the moles) to placing Wrigley's Juicy Fruit gum in a tunnel (supposedly, the smell is similar to the scent of a female, and males can't resist getting all gummed up with the stuff). One research study concluded that castor oil repels moles. There are commercial castor oil repellents on the market, but you can easily make your own. Mix one-eighth cup (one ounce) of castor oil (available at most pharmacies) with a gallon of warm water and add few drops of dish detergent to help persuade the oil and water to mix. This nontoxic concoction can be sprayed or sprinkled; a gallon covers about three hundred square feet.

But if you can't convince a mole to move its underground operation elsewhere, you could try repeating (and repeating) "Moles are beneficial," as you tamp down and smooth over their telltale tunnels and tailings.

Opossum

Latin name: *Didelphis marsupialis*
Description: 30 inches long, including 12-inch tail; white, pointed face; gray body fur; naked tail.
Habitat: Near marshes and streams, also farmland, towns, cities, suburbs, forests.

The unassuming opossum could claim the title of most unique mammal in North America. Several things set the opossum apart from the rest: it is our only marsupial (pouched animal); it has a prehensile (grasping) tail, more teeth than any other land mammal (fifty small, sharp ones), and opposable thumbs (on the hind feet); and it has the shortest gestation (a mere twelve to thirteen days).

For all its uniqueness, the opossum is generally considered a dim-witted little beast. This characteristic, along with its tendency to be active at night and its taste for carrion, are the reason why most of the opossums we see are dead ones along roadways. Its keen sense of smell leads it to dine upon other unfortunates on asphalt, and its tiny brain apparently doesn't register the approach of motor vehicles on its table. Thus the opossum ends up embodying the adage "You are what you eat."

This animal is not limited to roadkill meals, however. It has a taste for nearly everything it comes across: insects, mushrooms, corn, fruit, baby birds and eggs, worms, snakes, frogs, and small animals like mice and moles. Nor is it particular about where it sleeps. Although it stays within a limited territory, any drainpipe, abandoned burrow, woodpile, hollow tree or log, thicket, or space under a porch will do. Only a mother with young tends to use the same place for more than a day.

The opossum may fight or flee if attacked, but if cornered it does what it is famous for: it plays possum. The animal's eyes glaze and it drops to the ground, tongue lolling from mouth, teeth bared. This catatonic state is an involuntary response to danger and lasts anywhere from a few minutes to a couple of hours, after which the animal comes to as suddenly as it had "died from fright," regains its feet, and waddles away. (The ruse works because most of the opossum's potential predators are hunters who kill their meal rather than scavenge it.)

Because they are easy prey, opossums rarely live more than two years in the wild. Nevertheless, the species has survived fifty million years, since the time of the dinosaurs. North America's oldest and most primitive mammal continues to thrive, including in the Northwest, where it is a non-native. Its survival strategy is simple: fecundity. Opossums simply produce more opossums faster than they can be killed off.

Opossum mating has been the subject of folklore. Because the male has a forked penis and because the only obvious double opening in the female's body is her nostrils, it was once assumed that she was impregnated through the nose. (Her babies landed in her pouch, of course, when she bent over and sneezed them into it.) The real story is not quite—but nearly—as bizarre.

The male mounts the female, who does indeed have a forked vagina that nicely matches his sex organ. Donald and Lillian Stokes's *A Guide to Animal Tracking and Behavior* states that impregnation occurs only if the couple falls over on their right sides. Opossums that remain upright or fall to the left during mating are less likely to become parents.

The female gives birth just twelve to thirteen days later, although her young are still little more than embryos. The tiny mammals look like pink worms or grubs. They are less than half an inch in length, and the average litter of sixteen could fit in a teaspoon.

The young must make a treacherous journey up the mother's abdomen and into her fur-lined pouch. Prior to their birth, the mother has licked the area, and this trail of wet fur apparently helps guide the babies. Although their eyes, ears, hind legs, and tails are not fully formed, their front limbs are well enough developed to allow the young to drag themselves, hand over hand, through their mother's fur.

An opossum may give birth to more babies than she has nipples inside her pouch. Only those fortunate enough to find one of the thirteen teats will survive. Once the young have attached themselves, the nipples swell to fit their mouths and they stay attached as they develop. After about two months, the babies finally release the nipples and begin to venture outside the pouch, although they return to nurse. Young opossums gain independence at about three and a half months, making it possible for the mother to have two litters in a season.

The opossum may not be the fastest, smartest, or most beautiful animal in North America—but it *is* the only marsupial we've got.

Pacific Treefrog

Latin names: *Hyla regilla* or *Pseudacris regilla*

Description: To 2 inches long; often green, but variously colored; skin bumpy; black stripe from snout to shoulders; bulbous toe tips.

Habitat: Grass or low shrubs (rarely trees); ponds, seeps, wet meadows, slow streams, marshlands, woodlands.

The Pacific treefrog is a movie star. When Hollywood directors need the *ribbet* of frogs for background sound in a film, the treefrog is a natural. It's readily accessible (the frog's range extends down into California), and it trills loudly for several months during its breeding season. Thus, the harmonies of Pacific treefrogs have been heard in movies and television shows set in places where these amphibians would never be found—Amazon jungle, Maine woods, Louisiana bayou. (Filmmakers have much less regard for the importance of habitat than do the frogs themselves.)

But outside of movie theaters, here in the Pacific Northwest, the singing frogs you hear are probably this same species. Our other frogs are quieter and their musical seasons briefer. The introduced bullfrog is a notable exception to this, but its deep, droning *jug-o-rum* call is easily distinguished from the treefrog's higher-pitched *ribbet* or *kreeck-ek*.

Male treefrogs sing for sex from February to June. A female attracted to the commotion is seized from behind by one of the troubadours; he clings to her until she releases her eggs, which he then fertilizes. The jelly-encased eggs hatch into tadpoles in about three weeks and these metamorphose into miniature froglets about two months later. The treefrogs' relatively quick transformation from their aquatic stage to being able to travel abroad allows them to breed in ephemeral ponds. The skin of treefrogs also secretes a waxy substance that helps keep them from drying out and allows them to travel some distance from water. Any small frog in your yard is likely to be a Pacific treefrog. Regardless of its color, which is highly variable and depends upon its background, the treefrog can be identified by the dark stripe that runs from its snout, through its eyes, and down its shoulders, and by the tiny round pads at the tips of its toes.

If you catch a treefrog to observe it more closely, it will be more comfortable (as will any other amphibian) if you first get your hands wet. Once it's in hand, let it stretch out its hind legs so you can keep an easier grip around its middle. Or you can "hypnotize" a frog (and sometimes a toad) by turning it over and gently rubbing its belly for several seconds. Give it a gentle poke or clap your hands to wake it up. Scientists disagree on exactly why this works, but it usually does.

Scientists are also debating the appropriate name of this species; there is currently no consensus on whether it should be referred to as *Hyla regilla* (Pacific treefrog) or *Pseudacris regilla* (Pacific chorus frog). Of greater importance is the scientific discussion over what has caused an alarming increase of deformities in this species. Recent studies point to a parasite known as a trematode that embeds itself in the developing tissue of tadpoles, resulting in numerous flipperlike appendages instead of legs. But since the presence of trematodes is not new, the larger question is why the treefrogs are apparently now more vulnerable to their attack.

The deformities are especially ominous in light of the worldwide plummet of various amphibian populations.

There is general scientific agreement that habitat destruction is the main cause of the decline in frog, toad, and salamander numbers. And certainly introduced species (such as bullfrogs, in the Northwest) prey on native species, while having few predators of their own. Beyond that, many factors are being studied in an attempt to understand amphibian die-offs. Various studies implicate nitrogen compounds in agricultural fertilizers, a thinning ozone layer, fungal or algal infestations, and chemical pesticides. Different species may be affected by different causes or combinations of causes.

From microscopic viruses to global climate change, researchers are trying to piece together what is killing the amphibians. What they learn, combined with habitat conservation, may prevent a future where the only place to hear frogs call is at the movies.

Eastern Cottontail Rabbit

Latin name: *Sylvilagus floridanus*
Description: 18 inches long; upper fur grayish brown to reddish
brown; white or yellowish undersides; white underside of tail visible when
animal hops; often has white mark on forehead.
Habitat: Fields, open woodlands, suburbs, meadows, thickets, pastures, farmlands.

I f you see a bunny on your lawn or in your garden, it is more likely to be the introduced eastern cottontail than the native brush rabbit (*S. bachmani*). As their name implies, brush rabbits demand a dense brushy habitat and rarely stray far from it. (Nor are they found in Washington; the Columbia River appears to be the northernmost border for the brush rabbit.) But the eastern cottontail is less persnickety about its habitat and more likely to be seen out in the open.

Although you may see rabbits during the day, particularly if it's overcast, they are more likely to visit your yard at night. Eastern cottontails are active from dusk to dawn and spend their daylight hours resting. Unlike their European cottontail relations, North American cottontails don't dig burrows. Instead, they while away the daylight hours in a shallow depression called a form, which is usually hidden by an overhanging branch or some other cover. (The locally notorious "San Juan rabbit" might seem to be an exception to this because it digs burrows. But this species is actually the European rabbit, *Oryctolagus cuniculus,* which was introduced to the Puget Sound island by a lighthouse keeper. Because rabbits avoid swimming if they can, this destructive species has fortunately not spread to the mainland.)

The eastern cottontail, purposely released as a game animal in several areas in Washington and Oregon, has established itself in the Northwest. It eats an awesome variety of vegetation, including dandelions, grasses, clover, alfalfa, fruits and berries, and the bark of trees and shrubs. It will also go after lettuce, cabbage, beans, and other garden veggies. But contrary to popular belief (and Bugs Bunny cartoons), your carrots are safe from its raids: eastern cottontails do not dig for their meals.

It's been said that it's easier to list what a rabbit does not eat rather than what it does, so the cottontail's larger problem is not finding food but avoiding *becoming* food. The rabbit's extensive enemies list includes coyotes, owls, hawks, domestic dogs and cats, bobcats, foxes, and long-tailed weasels, as well as human hunters.

Because they are especially vulnerable when out feeding, rabbits have evolved a strategy that allows them to eat quickly yet fully digest their fibrous food later in the safety of their forms. Eastern cottontails, like pikas and some other small vegetarian mammals, void soft pellets and then reingest them to derive maximum nutrition from their meals. Hard, dry pellets of waste material are also voided, often when the animal feeds away from its form.

Rabbits stay within their own specific home ranges, where they are familiar with escape routes and the locations of their forms and feeding places. But they are not territorial creatures, and their ranges may overlap. Females are dominant in rabbit culture except when they are in estrus. The males within an area establish a hierarchy, and the most dominant, aggressive males mate more often with the females. Bunny machismo is demonstrated by threatening grass-scratching with forepaws and perhaps a chase; the rabbits rarely actually fight.

Both males and females are promiscuous. Their courtship consists of his running at her and her leaping over him and variations on this theme. Either one may spray the other with urine during foreplay. The actual mating, which is brief, stimulates ovulation in the female. After a gestation of nearly a month, she gives birth to four or five young in a shallow nest that she has lined with dry grasses and soft fur plucked from her chest and belly. She also creates a similar soft, warm covering that she pulls over the young when she leaves them. During the day she stays near the nest; at night she uncovers the nest a few times to feed the young and hides them again.

The female may have three or even four litters in one year. Just before giving birth she releases a sexually alluring scent (pheromone) that attracts males, and immediately after giving birth she is ready to mate again. The ability to "breed like rabbits" is a survival strategy. Fecundity is the cottontail's counterbalance against being appetizing, relatively defenseless cuisine.

Striped Skunk

Latin name: *Mephitis mephitis*

Description: Up to 32 inches long, including tail up to 11 inches; face black and narrow, with small eyes and ears; thin white line runs up nose and between eyes; black overall, with two white stripes that join at head and tail and are separate along back.

Habitat: Woodlands, fields, meadows, suburbs, towns.

We smell skunks far more often than we see them. This is not only because they are active from dusk to dawn, when we are less likely to be out and about, but also because they are strong candidates for roadkill. The little stinkers simply don't realize that their impressive weaponry does not intimidate cars.

All members of the weasel clan have well-developed musk glands, but the skunk has raised this trait to a high art. Like a kung fu master, the skunk travels peaceably through the world, secure in the knowledge of its own powers. When danger threatens, it employs its weapon only as a last resort. Before a skunk sprays, it gives its adversary an opportunity to back down and save face. A threatened skunk will arch its back and raise its tail to better advertise its warning colors, it may chatter its teeth, and when really worked up it may stamp the ground with its forefeet. By the time it curls its body in a U-shape and completely raises its tail facing the intruder, it is too late.

Twin nipples usually tucked into the anus are everted and, looking over its shoulder, the provoked skunk lets fly with an amazingly well-aimed shot of a sulfurous N-butyl mercaptan in an oily, amber fluid. This can travel over fifteen feet, and can be employed either as a mist or in jets, as the situation requires. And the skunk can direct the spray not only over either shoulder but also to either side, in front of or behind itself, and even above itself in order to hit its target—which is its opponent's face. In addition to the fetid, overpowering odor, the liquid burns the eyes, can temporarily blind, and often produces nausea.

The skunk's elaborate warning ritual, which may also include abrupt charges at the adversary, evolved not through some ancient mustelid family code of honor, but because a completely discharged skunk is defenseless. The animal can produce only so much ammunition at a time—enough for five or six sprays—and rebuilding the supply takes a while, so the skunk prefers to preserve it if possible.

A tomato-juice or vinegar bath is often prescribed for chagrined dogs who have challenged the peaceful warrior, but Larry Mueller offered a more effective bath alternative in his article, "De-skunking the Dog" (*Outdoor Life*, October 1977): Mix one-fourth cup baking soda and a teaspoon of liquid dish soap with a quart of three percent hydrogen peroxide (available in drugstores). Another home remedy Mueller recommends as superior to tomato juice is to pass the offending object, be it clothes or pet, through the cool smoke of a fire for just a couple of minutes. The acidic creosote in the smoke binds with the alkaline mercaptan to neutralize it.

Aside from raising a stink from time to time as need be, the skunk spends its waking hours waddling about, seeking sustenance. Although the bulk of its diet is usually insects, it is an omnivore apt to devour rodents, turtle and bird eggs, crayfish, garbage, carrion, and fruit.

One of the few animals that will eat an adult skunk is the great horned owl, which seems to have little or no sense of smell. Like people overly fond of garlic, great horned owls tend to exude the noticeable odor of their favorite dish.

Young skunks are particularly vulnerable to owl attack. A litter of skunks usually numbers four or five, and their all-important markings are evident on their hairless skin at birth. The mother keeps them in a den or underground burrow until they are about two months old. They learn to hunt by following her, single file, as she makes her nightly rounds. From an early age the babies practice their moves, stamping their little feet and raising their tails. By the time they leave their mother's care, the young have gained the assurance of those who are well versed in the ways of self-defense.

Rufous Hummingbird

Latin name: *Selasphorus rufus*
Description: 3½ inches; males mostly cinnamon-colored with iridescent red throat patches; females and immatures have green backs, white bellies, rufous sides.
Habitat: Gardens, forest edges, mountain meadows in bloom.

It's hard to imagine anyone disliking hummingbirds. Who could resist? Hummers are cute, they're colorful, and they're zippy. One of the Pacific Northwest's most common is the rufous hummingbird. The male is easily identified: he's rusty brown and has a glittering red throat patch or gorget (named after the piece of armor that protected a knight's throat). The female and the young are mostly green, and for this reason people often assume they belong to a different species.

The little birds' return from Mexico, usually in March, is a hopeful sign of spring. Males arrive in the Northwest early in the month, followed by females a few weeks later. Folklore once insisted that hummers hitched rides on migrating geese, tucked amongst their feathers. But this smallest of birds travels under its own power. It also boasts an extremely mobile shoulder joint that allows it to hover by moving its wings in a rapid figure-eight. Hummers can fly backward or forward, drop into steep dives, and even briefly fly upside down. The one thing hummingbirds cannot do is glide.

By May, the males are showing off their flight skills and plumage in aerial performances designed to dazzle the females. Once he's found an audience, an amorous male repeatedly rockets hundreds of feet up into the air, then slingshots back down, wings whirring and gorget flashing. He brakes just inches from the female so she can get a good look, and then he loops

back upward. If his
blitzkrieg works, the two will mate.
They then go their separate ways, she to raise
his offspring and he to attempt to wow other females.

The mother-to-be weaves a tiny nest only an inch and a half across, made from the stuff of fairy tales: silk from spiderwebs, woven around plant down and fuzzy moss or lichens. The two eggs she lays are about the size of pinto beans, from which hatch black, wrinkled, naked babies that have been compared to raisins.

The female leaves her nestlings only to eat. Upon her return, she shares the bounty with them, although her feeding method can make human observers queasy. The mother plunges her darning-needle beak down a gaping throat with such thrust that she seems likely to puncture her baby. Like many bird parents, she initially feeds her young regurgitated food, but they soon graduate to solids in the form of insects. These the mother catches on the wing, procures from their hiding or feeding places inside plants, or plucks from spiderwebs (both the arachnid's victims and the spider itself are fair game).

Hummers continue to feed on insects and spiders into adulthood, though their attraction to flower nectar is more famously known. A solution of four parts water to one part sugar approximates nectar, and many people offer this in hummingbird feeders. (Adding red dye to the mixture is unnecessary and introduces potentially harmful chemicals to the hummers. The blaring-red plastic portions of commercial feeders are purposely colored to attract the birds.) *Never* substitute honey or other sweeteners for sugar; these can become lethal to the birds.

A male rufous will not defend a mate or even his own eggs, but the feisty pipsqueak *does* defend his favorite food source from other hummers. You can't blame him. A hummingbird's voracious metabolism requires it to eat nearly its own weight in nectar each day. Rufous hummingbirds feed fourteen to eighteen times an hour while they are awake. At night they often drop into a torpor that lowers their temperature, thereby slowing their metabolic rate and allowing them to conserve energy. It is said that when they are active, hummers are constantly only a few hours from starvation.

It must be a hummingbird's small size that makes its indignant squeaks and belligerent darting defense of a choice feeding spot so comic. The same sort of rudeness in scrub jays or starlings just isn't endearing. Despite that audacity (or maybe because of it), hummers are the birds that charm us all.

Dark-eyed Junco

Latin name: *Junco hyemalis*

Description: To 6 inches; head brown or gray, darker in males than females; white belly; gray-brown back; gray-brown tail, except for white feathers on either side.

Habitat: Woodlands, meadows, brushy areas, stream banks, suburban yards.

If you have a bird feeder, especially a tray-style one, you've no doubt made the acquaintance of dark-eyed juncos. These birds recognize a good deal when they see one, and they tend to be regulars at backyard feeders, especially in winter.

During the cold season, juncos form flocks that travel throughout a small feeding territory. The group stays more or less together during the day and may follow a regular feeding circuit. The members also tend to roost together, often returning to the same roosting site night after night. Juncos have no objection to being with other bird species, and they may meld into mixed flocks that include chickadees, finches, and other birds.

Juncos practice a definite pecking order within their species in which males are dominant over females and adults are dominant over juveniles. This order is enforced with certain displays that you, just like a junco, can learn to recognize. In a pecking-attack, the dominant bird lunges at a subordinate, its head and body stretched out horizontally. The subordinate usually has the good sense to get out of the way, but if it doesn't, the other bird may peck it.

Another aggressive display is the head-dance. (This behavior can also be sexually suggestive, depending on the time of year and the gender of the birds involved.) Two birds, facing one another, repeatedly lift and lower their bills, as if nodding at one another. If they really get torqued off, the birds may lift off a bit in order to claw at one another, but usually they are able to resolve their differences with the head-dance alone. Either sex may initiate pecking-attacks or head-dancing, but only males seem to engage in flight-pursuit, one aerial chase after another.

Come spring, males use this same flight-pursuit technique on females. Some birds will remain in their wintering grounds, if there is enough suitable woodland for nest habitat. Other birds head for breeding grounds in conifer forests, sometimes at higher elevations. The males generally arrive first, and then chase the females when they arrive. Males also sing to attract a mate and spread and droop their wings. A mutually attracted pair show off their white feathers to one another by fanning their tails as they hop about with drooping wings.

Once they have mated, the task of making the nest falls to the female, although the male may offer dried grass, twigs, or bark. The nest is typically in a shallow depression on the ground, sheltered by overhanging vegetation and often situated against a bank, brush pile, rock outcropping, or some other upright structure. The female lays three to five eggs and incubates them without help from the male. When the young hatch after twelve or thirteen days, the male assumes his parental duties. The parents deliver food to their babies an average of eight times an hour. At first the young require regurgitated insects, but they soon graduate to soft insects and perhaps a few seeds. The parents solicitously remove the legs and wings of large insects before delivering them to the gaping jaws of their offspring.

The young birds are ready to fledge three weeks after hatching, although, like many ground-nesting birds, they are able to run long before they can fly. As the first clutch leaves the nest, they are attended by their father, while the mother prepares for a second brood. The birds remain on their breeding grounds until seasonal changes trigger the return to their wintering area.

Juncos are the original "snowbirds" (not the retirees who go to California or Florida for the winter). They earned this nickname not only because of their migration from Canada to snowy Eastern U.S. backyards but also because of their coloration ("dark skies above, snow below"). Because that coloration varies somewhat in different geographic areas, juncos were once classified as belonging to different species. Today they are recognized as one species, but the races are still sometimes identified by the old common names (such as "Oregon junco" for the Northwest's dark-hooded form). Despite their varying colors, juncos are united across the country in their appreciation of a free lunch. If you put out seeds for the birds, juncos will be among the crowd that accepts your kind offer.

Sharp~Shinned Hawk

Latin name: *Accipiter striatus*

Description: 10 to 12 inches; brown back and wings; lighter undersides barred with brown lines; relatively short, broad wings; long tail. Very similar to Cooper's hawk, but with a square-tipped tail that sometimes appears notched instead of the Cooper's more rounded tail.

Habitat: Forests, especially coniferous but also deciduous and mixed; often near clearings; sometimes seen in suburban neighborhoods.

The first sharp-shinned hawk I saw was at a raptor rehabilitation center, recuperating from a broken wing. Intrigued by this diminutive hawk, about the size of a jay, I looked it up in a bird book when I got home and learned that the "sharpie" was the smallest of the accipiters, a group of hawks that feed primarily on other birds. Its habitat is woodlands, where, although not often seen, it is especially common at the edge of clearings.

The second sharp-shinned I saw apparently hadn't read the same book, because it was sitting in a tree near my backyard bird feeder. The smaller birds had obviously noticed it before I had. Not a single well-fed junco nor house finch was anywhere to be seen. When the thwarted hawk flew off, I assumed it was returning to its presumably more-productive woodland.

But a week or so later my husband, Tim, looking out our kitchen window, saw a sudden explosion of feathers as the sharpie nailed a pine siskin that was flying toward the feeder. As the hawk began regularly returning to pick off my fatted songbirds, I consulted other bird books. One said that sharp-shins sometimes hunt at a number of neighborhood feeders, patrolling them like trap lines. Another mentioned that they usually

choose a particular perch near their hunting grounds, on which they pluck and devour their catch. This perch might be a stump or a rock and is sometimes called a "butcher's block." In my backyard, the butcher's block was a wooden post located conveniently near the feeder. Some days I could tell by the quantity of newly deposited feathers surrounding the post and the bits of down still sticking to it that the hawk had made an early morning kill while I'd been sleeping.

This tendency to kill other birds, even some larger than itself, earned the sharpie the description of "murderous little villain" in *Birds of America*, published in 1936. It was "relentless," and "a little demon" that attacked in a "blind fury." The book explained that there were "good" and "bad" birds and that the sharp-shinned, along with its fellow accipiters the Cooper's hawk and the goshawk, "deserve destruction."

Some people today might still agree with *Birds of America*. It can be tough to see coddled songbirds turned into fast food for a marauding hawk. But Tim and I found our sharpie so interesting we didn't begrudge it the occasional pine siskin or junco (though I did hope some of my favorites, like the chickadees and goldfinches, would continue to elude it).

Although the personal habits of sharp-shins are not as well known as those of most of the other hawks, it generally lays four or five eggs, which the female incubates for about a month while her mate brings her food. He continues to bring home the birdies after the young have hatched. The female may eventually help him hunt, especially if he has difficulty keeping up with the daily demand of two helpings of sparrow-sized birds for each family member.

After their offspring leave the nest, the parents continue to feed them. The youngsters finally try to hunt on their own when the adults cut back on the handouts. But intercepting and dispatching a moving target is a learned skill, and the young continue to rely on their parents for a while. About the time the hawks become independent in the fall, songbirds begin migration and are probably easier to take advantage of, which may ease the young sharpie's transition to adulthood.

The sharpie who visits us spends only the colder parts of the year patrolling our feeder, and each year we wait to see if it will return. When it does, we watch the life-and-death drama unfold outside our kitchen window as the sharpie dodges through the tree branches and lands on its butcher block with victim in talon.

American Robin

Latin name: *Turdus migratorius*

Description: About 10 inches; reddish orange breast; dark head with white outline around eye; gray back; yellow legs and beak. Female lighter in color than male.

Habitat: Forests and edges, urban and suburban areas, farmlands, parks, orchards.

The American robin is generally so beloved that it's startling to read John James Audubon's description of them as "fat and juicy" birds that "afford excellent eating." Long before laws were passed that prohibit killing most birds, the great ornithologist sampled many of his subjects.

In his day, Audubon's choice of cuisine was not considered a gastronomical oddity. In 1841, he wrote of the robins' fall migration into the Southern states: ". . . their presence is productive of a sort of jubilee among the gunners, and the havoc made among them with bows and arrows, blowpipes, guns, and traps of different sorts is wonderful. Every gunner brings them home by bagsful, and the markets are supplied with them at a very cheap rate. Several persons may at this season stand round the foot of a tree loaded with berries, and shoot the greater part of the day, so fast do the flocks of Robins succeed each other."

The robins' annual fall and spring migrations are not as obvious in the Northwest as they are in other parts of the country, though they do occur. The robins who claim territory in our backyards in spring move perhaps a few hundred miles to the south by winter. Meanwhile, robins who spend the summer in the mountains or farther north have moved here. So, although we see robins year-round, they are not necessarily the same birds in each season.

They're also more noticeable in spring and summer because their behavior changes with the changing weather. In the colder months, robins usually abandon backyards and head for the woods, where they gather in large flocks rather than in pairs or family groups. Even their diet changes. In winter they seek mostly berries and other plant foods instead of the earthworms and insects abundant in the warmer months.

Come springtime, the returning robins make themselves obvious. Males usually arrive first and stake out their territories. They proclaim their ownership in rousing song, which warns off other males and intrigues available females. Robins have a greater fidelity to last year's territory than to last year's mate, but a couple may reunite because each is faithful to the old neighborhood.

The work of nest-building falls mostly to the female, who weaves together twigs, dead leaves, and grasses. She requires mud to finish the nest and if she does not find it readily, she might create it by stepping into water and then into dirt. She carries the mud in her beak and plasters it on the inside of her cup-shaped nest. Then, sitting inside the nest, she turns round and round, tamping the mud into place with her body and shaping it to fit her comfortably. She may add a layer of fine grasses or moss before laying her (usually four) eggs.

Although they can be white, usually the eggs are a color so unique it has come to be called robin's-egg blue. When the ugly, pink, bald babies hatch out of those beautiful eggs, the parents are kept busy stuffing food into four gaping maws. One researcher determined that each nestling packs in three pounds of food in the two weeks it sits in the nest, which works out to about fourteen feet of earthworms per chick.

Robins appear to find those many earthworms by cocking their heads as if listening to underground digging. But research has shown that they are actually watching the ground, waiting for the twitch of a grass blade or any other slight movement that might reveal the presence of an insect or a worm. After two hectic weeks, the young robins are fledged. Now the father assumes complete responsibility for them, teaching them the finer points of food-finding, while the mother lays and hatches a second brood. The first brood may stick around and help feed their voracious siblings.

As might be assumed from their large broods, the mortality rate of robins is high, especially in the first year. But, happily for them, their habitat requirements neatly match those favored by humans. As long as lawns with earthworms and nest-holding trees and shrubs remain popular, the robin will be one of our most common species.

European Starling

Latin name: *Sturnus vulgaris*

Description: 8 inches; iridescent black plumage, covered with white spots in winter; stubby tail.

Habitat: Towns, suburbs, parks, fields.

March 16, 1890, is a day that lives in avian infamy. That's the day a man named Eugene Schieffelin released starlings into New York's Central Park. The goal of his organization, the American Acclimatization Society, was to introduce into America all the birds found in the works of William Shakespeare. And in *Henry IV,* unfortunately, the Bard had mentioned starlings. These birds are well adapted to their homelands of England and Eurasia, but here in America, they are aggressive immigrants who outcompete and displace native birds.

Schieffelin was not the only person to introduce starlings to America. *Birds of Oregon,* published in 1940, briefly noted the European starling as a species that had become "extinct" in the Pacific Northwest. It explained that "in 1889 and 1892, the Portland Song Bird Club released thirty-five pairs of Starlings in Portland. These birds established themselves and remained for a number of years, but some time about 1901 . . . disappeared, which, in light of the trouble with this species in the Eastern States, was a fortunate thing." But the Northwest's grace period was short. By the 1950s the pushy starling was here to stay, having gradually colonized its way across the country from New York.

There are those who admire the bird's talent for mimicry, or its iridescent coloring, or the white spots that adorn its winter plumage—the "stars" that starlings were named for. Some also appreciate the bird's appetite for introduced slugs and other garden pests. But orchardists, vineyardists, and livestock owners who see their fruit or their animal feed set upon by huge flocks do not think kindly of starlings. Neither do birders, who know that starlings usurp the nests of flickers, bluebirds, wrens, and other cavity-nesters. The sheer noise and copious amount of slimy waste created by big flocks also cause havoc in towns and cities.

But starlings see themselves in a different light—quite literally. Studies have shown that, unlike people, starlings are able to see in the ultraviolet range. Apparently most birds can see richer hues than humans because they have four color receptors compared to our three; they see a wider part of the color spectrum. It's a little humbling to realize that even the lowly starling perceives the world more brilliantly than the most-attuned human artist.

The females seem to use this ability to help determine which male is most desirable, recognizing colors in his plumage that we can't see. Once the birds have paired off and established a nest site, the female lays four to six pale blue eggs. She may also lay one in a neighboring starling's nest, if the residents are temporarily away, so that they will assume it is their own and raise her offspring. The female incubates the eggs most of the time, but the male takes over for a small part of each day. Both deliver worms and insects after the young hatch. Around twenty days after hatching, the off-spring are ready to leave the nest and forage on their own.

A starling has jaws that are said to work "backward." Its jaw muscles allow it to grasp objects, but they also give it superior strength to pry things apart. In its search for insects, a starling will poke its closed bill into the grass of a lawn, then spring open its jaws, tearing the sod apart. This is yet another habit unlikely to endear the starling to suburbanites, and can be added to the list of that bird's detrimental activities. Most people would probably agree that it's a shame Eugene Schieffelin succeeded where the genteel folk of the Portland Song Bird Club failed. But, like many other European immigrants that the original inhabitants of this continent would arguably have been better off without, the starling is here to stay.

Spotted Towhee

Latin name: *Pipilo maculatus* (formerly *P. erythrophthalmus*)

Description: 8 inches; dark head; rusty sides, rest of belly white;
dark wings speckled with white; dark tail with white markings at tips' corners;
red eyes (color not obvious in dim light). Males darker than females.

Habitat: Thickets, brush near open areas, forest clearings,
yards and gardens with concealing bushes.

At first glance, the spotted towhee might look like the impossible offspring of a dark-eyed junco and a robin. The towhee has the same dark-hooded head as the Northwest junco, combined with the rusty coloring of the robin (although this is found on the towhee's sides, not across the entire breast). That rusty-orange coloration earned the bird its former name of "rufous-sided towhee." But when taxonomists determined that our Western bird was not the same species as the Eastern version, they reassigned it its older common name of "spotted towhee," which calls attention to the white spots sprinkled on its wings. A regional subspecies, which tends to be a brighter orange than other towhees, is still often called the "Oregon towhee."

Whatever you call them, these birds are year-round residents in the Pacific Northwest. They literally scratch out a living, using a peculiar two-legged backward kick. Towhees rummage around in duff and dried leaves on the ground, kicking through the litter in their search for insects. These little birds can make quite a rustling racket, and some birders use this to help them locate towhees. Birders also listen for the bird's *t'hee* call, which led to the name towhee.

In spring, the male shows off his white spots to any nearby female, raising his wings and fluffing his feathers to present them at greatest advantage. The towhee's fiery red eyes are such a striking color that it seems he should just wink at the female to win her over, but there's no accounting for taste: the female towhee is apparently more impressed by white spots. He also spreads his tail feathers so she can get a gander at their white corner markings. If she likes what she sees, the two will mate and seek an appropriate nest site.

Towhees are quite secretive about this location, perhaps because they usually nest on the ground rather than in a tree. The female makes the nest and does all the incubation, leaving her three to five eggs only when she needs to eat. She is stealthy in her departure, walking away from the nest site before taking to the air. She's equally circumspect when returning to the nest, landing nearby and then approaching under the cover of vegetation. If a human blunders near the nest, the mama bird will usually sit tight, allowing an approach within inches before she abandons her young. Then she may attempt to distract the interloper by feigning injury while moving away from the nest.

The male rarely comes near the nest at all until the young are hatched and in need of food. During the six or seven days while the female broods their hatched offspring, the male is the main insect-winner, but when the female stops brooding, she takes on the greatest portion of the food-gathering chore. The young can fly ten to twelve days after hatching, though their parents continue to feed them for perhaps a month.

Towhees can raise two broods a year, usually with the same mate. Sometimes the young they raise are not really their own, however. Towhees are a frequent host to the brown-headed cowbird, that parasitic interloper who lays her own eggs in the nests of other species, thereby forgoing the responsibility of raising them. Duped towhees incubate and then care for the young cowbird, which tends to outcompete its fellow nestlings for food.

If it raises its own offspring, the towhee family might stay together for the rest of the summer; during the winter, it may form a loose flock with other birds such as juncos and chickadees. Although towhees may join the other birds at a hanging backyard feeder, they prefer a feeder located on the ground or an area with some protective underbrush. There, using backward hops, they scuffle, scratch, and rustle up some grub.

Killdeer

Latin name: *Charadrius vociferus*

Description: To about 11 inches; twin black neck bands; cinnamon-colored rump and tail, especially conspicuous when bird flies.

Habitat: Farm fields, river estuaries, golf courses, airports, large lawns, pastures, fields, meadows, freshwater marshes and mudflats.

When she was just two years old, my daughter could identify the killdeer's call—but that ability had more to do with the bird's vociferousness than with Hallie's talent as a birder. Killdeers nest in the open field behind our house each summer, and we can hear their high *tir-eee* and *Dee, dee, dee!* alarm cries throughout the day, especially in the early morning and at dusk, and even during moonlit nights. (The classic "kill-deer, kill-deer" call that earned the bird its common name is usually made by courting males.)

This bird is so talkative that the second half of its Latin name is *vociferus*. The chicks have something to say even before they are hatched, and can be heard peeping at least two days before they begin breaking through their shells.

Killdeers are shorebirds, but they can stray far from shore. They are found on golf courses and airport fields, on plowed land and in pastures—basically anywhere they're likely to find insects and other small creatures to eat. The killdeer diet includes beetles, dragonflies, worms, mosquito larvae, ticks, grasshoppers, caterpillars, and ants.

They are swift fliers and runners. Characteristically, they'll run several steps, pause, then run again, heads bobbing. A killdeer tends to stand out on a grassy area, but its coloration blends in with a mottled background, and the two black bands on its neck break up its silhouette. The first clue that a killdeer is in the area often comes from its own announcement—*Dee!*—rather than from an actual sighting.

The eggs, although laid out in the open, are even harder to spot. Killdeer generally seek a shallow depression to use as a nesting site. The hollow is sometimes lined with a bit of gravel or some pebbles, but the parents don't seem to fuss much over their nest, and have been known to use an old road rut or even a flat rooftop. The four mottled eggs that are typically laid are so well camouflaged you can miss them even if you are looking directly at them.

The parents place the eggs so that the small ends are together in the middle of the nest. (It has been suggested that this way the eggs occupy as little space as possible.) Should they be moved, the adult birds will reposition them. But the parents are unlikely to let you disturb them. When an intruder comes too near the nest, whichever parent is closer will fake injury to draw attention to itself. Individual birds vary in their acting ability and technique. One might beat its wings against the ground and shriek in apparent desperation, another drag a spread wing or tail. Some flutter just beyond a predator's reach; others flounder, then suddenly recover and fly perfectly well, only to suffer an apparent relapse a short distance away.

The parents take turns incubating the eggs for nearly a month. If the sun is too hot, the adult will stand so that its shade covers the nest, often after wading into water to wet its belly feathers and then brushing the water onto the eggs. Within a few hours of hatching, the young are on their feet and ready to follow their parents. The adults don't bring food to their babies, but instead lead them to it. The mottled, downy young are as well camouflaged as were their eggs. Although they can run shortly after breaking through the shell, their usual response to danger is to freeze. The little puffballs hunker down, close their dark eyes, and remain motionless as their thespian parents perform the "wounded" routine. About twenty-five days after hatching, the young grow flight feathers and become independent.

Killdeer are year-round residents of the Pacific Northwest; the southern part of Oregon's Willamette Valley is one of their major wintering grounds. Our neighborhood killdeer leave the field behind our house, perhaps to join one of the large flocks that form in wintertime. As the days and nights cool, we become aware that the repetitious calls that had blended into summer's background sounds are missing, and then we know we won't hear another strident *dee, dee, dee!* until the following spring.

Northern flicker

Latin name: *Colaptes auratus*
Description: 11 inches; brown back, black-spotted breast, black bib, red under wings; male has red "mustache."
Habitat: Open woodlands, suburbs, farms, orchards, parks.

Among woodpeckers, the northern flicker is a bit of an eccentric. Like others in its family, the flicker has a bill that grows continuously so that it does not become worn down, and it has the strong claws and stiff tail feathers that allow woodpeckers to stand nonchalantly on the sides of trees. But unlike other woodpeckers, who typically confine their activities to the forests, the flicker is likely to be found on open ground—hunting for ants, or visiting a backyard suet feeder, or attempting to hammer out a nest under house eaves.

As a result of these habits, flickers are the most often seen woodpecker in the Northwest (and across the United States). Ornithologists once recognized three distinct species of these birds: the red-shafted flicker found west of the Rockies, the yellow-shafted found east of the Rockies, and the gilded of the Southwest. The differences among them are in their coloration: the salmon-red underwings and red moustache of our birds, the yellow underwings and black moustache of the yellow-shafted flicker, and the yellow underwings and red moustache of the gilded flicker. But because the birds can interbreed, it was decided in 1973 that they were actually one species with three races, all of which are now called the northern flicker.

Regardless of where they live or the color of their wings, all flickers have a long tongue and sticky saliva that allow them to collect ants. They consume more ants than any other bird in North America, and are often seen hopping or running about on the ground like a robin. They'll also eat beetles, wasps, grasshoppers, crickets, wood lice, caterpillars, grubs, and various other flying insects that they nab on the wing. In fall and winter, their fare is likely to include berries, nuts, seeds of such plants as grasses, clover, and ragweed, and suet from backyard feeders.

During the spring mating season, which generally begins in April, male flickers call attention to themselves by drumming. Hammering their bills against any resonant surface—tin roofs and drainpipes work as well as hollow trees or limbs—the males persistently announce themselves. Once his provocative message has attracted the attention of a female, the male flicker further impresses her with loud calls and by showing off his plumage. He parades before her with wings and tail spread, bowing and nodding. If she is appropriately impressed, the two will mate and begin the business of rearing a family.

Nesting flickers usually favor hollow trees, but they have been known to dig burrows in dirt banks even when trees were available. Both sexes create the nest, which may take a week or two, or they may refurbish an old nest. After making a two- to four-inch-wide entrance hole, they carve a tubular hollow about ten to thirty-six inches down into the tree. The female lays her eggs, usually six to eight, on a bed of wood chips at the bottom. Like chickens, flickers are "indeterminate layers" who, if some eggs are lost, will keep producing more until the right clutch number is reached. A relentless researcher once removed an egg a day from a flicker's nest, causing her to lay seventy-one eggs in seventy-three days.

Both parents incubate the eggs, with the female generally sitting during the day and the male on duty at night. The young are fed regurgitant, and they excrete their waste in tough little sacs that their parents remove to keep the nest clean. The young are independent after about a month. The flicker's old nest holes, like those of other woodpeckers, are often used by animals that would have difficulty excavating cavities on their own—

including screech owls, kestrels, buffleheads, and squirrels.

The northern flicker's distinctive undulating flight makes it one of the easiest birds to identify on the wing. The flicker beats its wings, heading upward, then briefly closes them to swoop downward in a roller-coaster motion. A distinguishing bright-white rump patch, visible when the bird is flying, also helps with identification. The northern flicker is not only the Pacific Northwest's most common woodpecker but—with its flight pattern, food habits, and coloration—also our most easily recognized.

American Kestrel

Latin name: *Falco sparverius*

Description: To 10½ inches; both sexes have double black stripes on face, rusty back and tail; males have blue-gray wings.

Habitat: Fields, pastures, open country, towns and cities.

A rose by any other name may be the same, but the sparrow hawk was definitely misnamed. For many years, that was the common name of the bird now called the American kestrel, despite the fact that it is not a hawk, nor are sparrows its preferred food.

The kestrel is a falcon and can be distinguished from its relative, the hawk, by its pointed and narrow wings. It is the smallest falcon, slightly larger than a robin, and one of the most beautifully marked. As with many birds of prey, the female is slightly larger than the male.

Although it *will* kill and eat sparrows, the kestrel feeds mainly on insects, especially grasshoppers during the summer, and also takes small mammals like mice; it hunts small birds only in the winter or when large insects are not available. The misleading name "sparrow hawk" was officially dropped in 1982, reducing confusion over the family connections and dietary preferences of the bird.

Most falcons seize their prey on the wing, but kestrels have an additional strategy. They face into the wind and hover in an updraft, scanning the ground for insects or mice. One naturalist reported hearing a hunting kestrel "squeak" as if trying to draw out a hidden mouse. When the bird spots its prey, it plunges to the ground for the kill, then takes the victim to its perch to consume it. Kestrels can often be seen along roadways, either hovering over fields and grassy areas or sitting on utility lines and fence posts.

In the spring, the male courts the perched female by flying high above her, crying a characteristic *killy killy killy*. She may join him in flight, or, more likely, will wait for him to drop down and perch beside her. They bow to one another, while the male continues his shrill call. When they are near a suitable nest site, perhaps an old woodpecker hole, he may bring her a food offering. The two perch side by side, again bowing and bobbing, before the female accepts the mouse or grasshopper from her new mate's talons.

After the four or five eggs are laid, the female does most of the month-long incubation, while the male continues to feed her. The downy white nestlings eat the mice and insects delivered to them for about three weeks, and after they leave the nest, the parents continue to feed them for a time. Unlike most young birds, juvenile kestrels can be identified as male or female by their coloration: the males sport beautiful blue-gray wings.

Kestrels are the only North American falcon that will readily nest in bird boxes. This willingness, along with their dietary preferences, has prompted the creation of "kestrel trails" along highways in several states. A grassy highway median supplies both abundant prey and perches and, with the addition of nest boxes, becomes an ideal place for kestrels to raise a family. Nest boxes, attached to the back of the green highway signs every mile or so, have created kestrel trails in Iowa, Minnesota, Missouri, Nebraska, Wisconsin, and Idaho, significantly boosting the kestrel populations in those states.

To the best of my knowledge, kestrel trails have not yet been established in either Washington or Oregon, but there is no reason why they wouldn't work as well here. Stuck in a traffic jam, which would you prefer to watch: a hovering kestrel scouting for grasshoppers, or the bumper in front of you?

Ring~Necked Pheasant

Latin name: *Phasianus colchicus*

Description: To 33 inches tall; body stout; long, tapering tail. Male: green head with patches of red (wattles) around eyes; bronze overall with iridescent green-blue ear-tuft feathers; most have white neck ring. Female: a plain sandy brown; shorter tail than male.

Habitat: Open spaces with brushy cover, riparian areas, fields, croplands, pastures, woodland edges.

I glanced out my bedroom window one morning to see a male ring-necked pheasant poking through the corn stubble of our backyard garden. Within a few moments, I also spotted a female, who blended in so well with the background I noticed her only when she moved. The two of them eventually stepped back through the open wooden gate into the field beyond. Until I saw them, I had no idea pheasants might be living in the little ten-acre field behind our house.

I was equally surprised the day I watched a male fly across a four-lane highway I was traveling. The highway was flanked by fields on either side, and the cock made it safely from one to the other. Pheasants like the brushy edges of open spaces, and they can still be found living on the margins of suburbs and highways. During the 1950s and '60s, sighting ring-necked pheasants along roads, in fields, and on farmlands was an everyday occurrence, but since that time habitat destruction and changes in farm policies have significantly lowered their populations.

As common as the birds might once have been here, they are not native to the Northwest, or even to North America. Ring-necks hail originally from China, and several tries were made before they were successfully introduced to the United States. George Washington imported some from England to Mount Vernon, but they were probably domesticated stock and did not thrive in the New World.

The first successful introduction of the large birds was here in the Northwest. In 1881, Judge Owen N. Denny, U.S. consul general in Shanghai, shipped wild ring-necked pheasants to Albany, Oregon. After claiming the Willamette Valley area, the birds spread out and were also transplanted to other areas of the country. Additional shipments added to their numbers, and ring-necked pheasants quickly became a popular game bird across America.

Pheasants are related to domestic chickens (as well as to quails and peacocks), and the males reveal that connection by their behavior in spring. They choose a conspicuous rock or other high point on their territory and, rising up on tiptoe, crow each morning just before dawn, flapping their wings with a sound like muffled applause. They are announcing their territory and attempting to entice females.

The male I saw from my bedroom window apparently had only one mate, perhaps because his territory was small. Before breeding season begins, females gather together in groups called harems, which will accept as their mate one male whose territory encompasses their normal feeding area. The male woos each female singly, often when she is briefly separated from the group. He struts before her, spreading wings and tail and tilting them toward her. The ear tufts on his head are raised, and the wattles around his eyes swell and become a brighter red. He might also find a piece of food and, jerking his head, point it out to her. When he eventually convinces her, she will squat and allow him to mount.

Each female usually makes a separate nest, although two may occasionally lay in the same one. The nest is a casual affair—just a shallow hole scratched into the ground, concealed by tall grass. It is often situated just outside the male's territory. Each female leaves the harem every two days or so to lay an egg, returning to the group afterward. When her entire clutch is laid, she will leave the group for the rest of the season. She incubates her eggs, usually around a dozen, for just over three weeks, leaving only once a day to feed. Once the young hatch, the family group travels about, the mother pointing out food to her young. They don't return to the nest, but instead the female broods the young at night, tucking them under her feathers.

The young eat only insects at first but soon graduate to adult fare, adding weed seeds, grains, nuts, and berries. Ring-necked pheasants also tend to dig up newly planted corn, peas, beans, and other vegetables—which means I may be seeing them again some spring, perusing our garden's bounty.

Swallows

Latin names: *Tachycineta bicolor* (tree swallow); *T. rustica* (formerly *Hirundo rustica*) (barn swallow); *Petrochelidon pyrrhonota* (formerly *Hirundo pyrrhonota*) (cliff swallow)

Description: To 6 inches, depending on species; slender body; long, pointed wings.

Habitat: Open forests, cliffs, bridges, farm fields, pastures, must be near water.

Although swallows return to the Northwest each spring as reliably as they do to Capistrano, our birds get a lot less hype. According to legend, cliff swallows arrive at the San Juan Capistrano Mission in southern California on March 19 each year. (The birds actually rely more on favorable weather than on a particular calendar date.)

It takes them a little longer to arrive in the Northwest, but by late March or early April, you may become aware of swooping and darting swallows slicing the air above you. Tree swallows are generally the first of their tribe to arrive. Unlike the

others, they can subsist on seeds and fruits while waiting for insects to hatch.

Different swallow species have different preferences, but swallows can be found on farms and in suburbs, in open forests and in open country. All demand an area that offers both a good supply of flying insects and a source of water. The open-mouthed birds intercept mosquitoes, flies, beetles, and wasps in midair. If you walk across an open field in high summer, you may be buzzed at close range by swallows snatching the insects your footsteps have disturbed, and if it's quiet enough you may even hear their beaks snapping.

Water is needed for on-the-wing drinks and baths. In addition, both cliff and barn swallows require mud for nest-building. (As their name implies, tree swallows nest in the hollows of trees.) Barn and cliff swallows roll mud into pellets with their beaks. They carry each pellet to the nest site—which in the case of the barn swallow could well be a barn, while for the cliff swallow (no surprise here) the side of a cliff works nicely. The barn swallow layers its nest with straw, but its cliff-dwelling cousin is a purist; its nest is made entirely of mud or clay. A mated pair of cliff swallows gathers hundreds of pellets to make their gourd-shaped nursery. Since it's much easier to repair an old home than build a new one, it's not surprising that such labor-intensive nests are used year after year.

Cliff swallows nest in large colonies, and they are not above stealing a few pellets from a neighbor's unsupervised construction site—or even taking over a completed home if possible. Their duplicity doesn't end there, however. Cliff swallows have a particularly high rate of brood parasitism. A female might slip into a momentarily vacant nest and lay an egg there to be raised by her unsuspecting neighbor. Or she might carry one of her own eggs next door in her beak. Her mate takes this a step further—actually pushing neighboring eggs out of their nests, apparently to make room for those that carry his genes. It seems that cliff swallows are not as virtuous as their mission-nesting reputation implies. It's been estimated that more than one-fourth of cliff swallow nests may be parasitized. Some wife-swapping goes on as well, although it's much more common for tree swallows than for cliff swallows to have liaisons with a non-mate.

Once the young hatch, they benefit from the cliff swallows' trait of nesting in colonies. Parents who have been unsuccessful in finding food can observe a neighbor arriving with insects and note which direction it came from. The colony is said to be an information center where less-successful parents can learn where good feeding areas are located.

About three weeks after hatching, the young have been raised, whether by their parents or by foster parents. By late summer, swallows gather in great flocks. They are one of the first birds to migrate, and they rendezvous before undertaking the long trip to South America. Swallows return to warmer and sunnier climes for the winter months, where their arrival is no doubt also avidly noted and appreciated.

American Goldfinch

Latin name: *Carduelis tristis*

Description: 5 inches. Breeding male bright yellow with black cap, black wings with two white bars, yellow shoulder patch, black and white tail. Winter adults and immatures brownish or grayish. Female dull olive-brown year-round.

Habitat: Weedy fields, pastures, marsh edges, roadsides, open areas, suburbs.

Goldfinches are the birds of summer. Not only do male American goldfinches sport a glorious sunshiny yellow, but because they nest late, these birds have more carefree summer days than do most songbirds.

During the warm months, the bright-yellow, black-capped male goldfinches are easy birds for the beginning birder to recognize. And goldfinches are birds of suburbia. They are not found in dense woods, but prefer open areas, especially weedy fields, pastures, and places where shrubs and low trees grow. They nest near sites that harbor thistles. So strongly is the goldfinch associated with the prickly plant that one of its older names is "thistle bird."

The thistle is the reason that the goldfinch is the last bird in North America to begin raising its young each season. While other birds are making nests and hatching their young during the spring, goldfinches have no such responsibilities, continuing their carefree existence until late June, July, or perhaps even August. Unlike most songbirds, who feed insects to their young, goldfinches primarily feed theirs regurgitated plant seeds, especially thistle seeds. The breeding cycle of the birds is timed to the appearance of the downy seed.

The female weaves a cup-shaped nest from grasses and other plants, a duty she seems to take most seriously. She adds spider silk and caterpillar webbing to bind it and lines it with cattail fluff, thistledown, or milkweed down. The result is a nest so tightly woven it can hold water. (It's even been claimed that the female must shield the nest with outstretched wings during rainstorms to prevent the young from drowning.) Because the female incubates the eggs and then stays with the young most of the time, the male feeds both her and the young. The fledglings leave the nest after about two or two and a half weeks. Toward the end of that time, the female begins to help the male feed them, though she occasionally still begs food herself, apparently having gotten used to the lifestyle.

Goldfinches change mates from year to year, the female seeming to be more attached to a nesting site than to any particular male. Before and after the breeding season, the birds are gregarious and tend to travel in flocks. Their flight is an undulating wave pattern: they travel from tree to tree as though on a roller-coaster ride without the coaster.

If you would like to attract these beautiful birds to your yard, try planting the seed flowers they prefer, such as sunflowers, cosmos, coneflowers, and zinnias. Consider setting aside a wildflower area with goldenrod, asters, dandelions, thistles, and milkweed; or offer Niger thistle seeds and sunflower seeds at a feeder during summer. Then, while you are relaxing in the hammock or firing up the barbecue on long warm afternoons, you can watch the carefree birds of summer.

Song Sparrow

Latin name: *Melospiza melodia*

Description: To 6 inches; back and head brown, streaked with black; broad gray eyebrow stripe; whitish breast streaked with brown, which converges near center of breast to form a dark spot.

Habitat: Forest edges, thickets, gardens, hedges, fields, meadows, marshes, along waterways.

When you're ready to tackle sparrow identification, the song sparrow is the place to start. For one thing, it is probably the most common sparrow in the Northwest, and for another, it's easy to identify once you know what to look for. The brownish streaks on its breast converge to form a central spot. And if the bird is in flight, watch for a pumping action of the tail.

As might be expected in a bird whose common name includes "song" and whose Latin species name is *melodia*, the male song sparrow is also easily recognized by his cheerful-sounding call. Thoreau interpreted the three short notes and buzzy trill as "Maids! Maids! Maids! Hang up your teakettle-ettle-ettle!" but other birders have suggested "Hip-hip-hip-hooray, boys, spring's here!" or "Pres-pres-pres-byteri-eri-erian!" or the more ecumenical "Peace-peace-peace unto you, my children." Doubtless the song has other connotations to the female bird.

Once she has been attracted into the male's territory by his song, he's liable to chase her about, often singing as he flies, and when perched, he flutters his wings provocatively. Song sparrows are known to be polygamous if a female's partner dies and in areas where females outnumber males. The birds seem to require thickets in their nesting territory, and often make use of blackberry brambles as nesting sites.

A pair may have as many as three broods a year. The first cup-shaped nest is usually on the ground, and although the pair may use this nest again, they are more likely to build subsequent nests higher up in a bush or tree, apparently to take advantage of the cover provided by the newly emerged leaves. The female lays three to five eggs, which she incubates for about two weeks.

When the first egg hatches, however, the chick that emerges might be a brown-headed cowbird rather than a song sparrow. The eggs of the two species are rather similar in size and markings, and song sparrows are one of the birds most frequently parasitized by cowbirds. The female cowbird makes no nest of her own but relies on the kindness of strangers to raise her young. After she lays an egg in the briefly unattended sparrow's nest, her parenting duties toward that chick are completed. Her young will likely hatch before the other eggs and will grow faster. Although the cowbird hatchling does not oust the young sparrows, it will outcompete them for the food delivered by their parents and, at the very least, reduce the amount they receive.

Like many ground nesters, the parents may perform a distraction display to lead potential predators from the vicinity of their nest. The song sparrow's version of this involves running about with tail lowered while holding up both wings. The sparrow young are out of the nest about five weeks after they hatch, but at this stage they are not quite ready for life on their own, so the male continues to tend them while the female prepares for their next brood.

No doubt the song sparrow's fecundity allows it to be so abundant, despite its favored status as a cowbird host. Song sparrows are one of North America's most widely distributed native birds. With that wide distribution comes a correspondingly high variation in coloration. When you travel outside the Pacific Northwest, you may find locals identifying some slightly different small brown bird with a spot on its breast as a song sparrow—there are dozens of variations on the theme. When in doubt, however, you can always confidently fall back on the old tactic of identifying any sparrowlike bird as an "LBJ"—a "little brown job."

American Crow

Latin name: *Corvus brachyrhynchos*
Description: 17 inches; black body with iridescent highlights; squared-off tail.
Habitat: Open areas such as farmlands, grassy areas, parks, yards; also woodlands, including specific roosts where thousands may gather.

Crows are the hooligans of neighborhood birds. They're brash, they talk too loud, and they swagger when they walk. They may show up in your backyard, but chances are they don't want your stinkin' birdseed, man. (Well, maybe some cracked corn or sunflower seeds—and the garbage in your trash can will do nicely.)

Few birds embody as much personality as do crows. These days, they're invariably described as cocky, brassy, smart, or clever. It's an improvement over earlier attitudes toward them, when they were considered evil and sinister, and a gathering of the dark birds was assigned the appellation "a murder of crows." As the early ornithologist John James Audubon noted, "almost every person has antipathy" toward crows. In the 1940s, tens of thousands of crows at a time were killed by the deliberate dynamiting of their evening roosts.

Certainly, the birds that generated such revulsion are not your typical songbirds. Still, songbirds they are, even if it's a stretch of the imagination to refer to their raucous calls as "songs." It's even more mind-bending to learn that crows use over twenty calls to relay information to one another. Different calls express actions such as courting, threatening, gathering together, and dispersing. A distinctive alarm cry calls every crow within earshot to "mob" an owl or hawk: the convening crows wheel above and swoop down upon the threat, eventually driving it away. (Likewise, crows themselves are mobbed by the smaller birds which could become their prey.)

A crow who discovers an intact dead animal too large to break into on its own may use a different call to summon reinforcements to help open up the carcass. Each crow also appears to have its own personal call that distinguishes it among its family. Incredibly, a bird separated from its mate may mimic the other's unique sounds, as if calling it home by "name." And crows have long been noted for their ability to imitate the sounds of machinery, water, and other animals, including ducks, dogs, cats, and humans.

Members of the crow family have the largest brains, in proportion to their body size, of any bird. Scientists have determined that crows can perform simple counting exercises, distinguish shapes such as circles, squares, and triangles, and solve various puzzles. It's also clear that these birds learn not only from from their own experiences but also by watching other crows. Once acquainted with the dangers of rifles, for example, they'll steer clear of them. And although they often feed on roadkill, they have the sense to get out of the way of oncoming traffic.

Birdwatchers in our region sometimes distinguish between the common American crow and the somewhat smaller "Northwestern crow" typically found on the coast, but most ornithologists now recognize them as slightly different races of the same species. Both races are thought to mate for life, though they might indulge in dalliances outside their primary relationship. The female is responsible for building the nest, a bulky contraption of sticks typically found in the high center of trees (the "crow's nest" position). The four or five eggs are thought to be incubated by both parents for about 18 days, and both feed the hatchlings.

A crow's diet includes insects, fruit, carrion, garbage, frogs, and seeds, especially corn. They may also occasionally raid other birds' nests, devouring eggs or nestlings. Like owls, they expel pellets containing the indigestible bits of shell, bone, or fur.

Like primates, crows have been known to use tools (such as sticks for probing and prying). By doing so, they engage in an activity that was once considered the exclusive domain of humans. Of course, you're unlikely to find a scientist who would liken a crow's intelligence to that of a person's, but the risk of anthropomorphizing didn't faze the Reverend Henry Ward Beecher. This eminent nineteenth-century orator once stated, "If men had wings and bore black feathers, few of them would be clever enough to be crows." To which I can only add: "Amen, Reverend, amen."

California Quail

Latin name: *Callipepla californica*

Description: 10 inches; mostly blue-gray and brown above; dark-edged belly feathers appear scalloped; black teardrop-shaped plum arcing from the forehead is larger in males.

Habitat: Grasslands, fields, brushy areas, stream valleys, and suburbs.

The California quail's motto might be "Safety in numbers." Then again, it could be "Why fly when you can run?" This compact bird is most often seen in a flock called a covey, and usually on the ground rather than in the air.

Because of their ground-hugging habit, where there are quail there will also be brush or thickets to shelter them. The birds can, however, fly swiftly for short distances, and they will use this method of escape as a last resort. Their short, rounded wings enable them to burst into flight from a standstill, and each member of a group is likely to light out in a different direction, further confusing an enemy. When they land, they keep running. Once the danger has passed, the scattered covey reconvenes, using an assembly call to find one another. Satisfied grunts and cackles are also in their vocal repertoire.

Quail are happily gregarious until springtime, when mating pairs prefer a little privacy. Previously mated couples tend to reunite to raise another family. A courting male bows to his partner, fluffs his body feathers, and may run at her with drooping wings and fanned tail feathers.

The female, impressed with this display, mates with the male and then finds an appropriate nest site—a spot concealed by grasses or shrubs, preferably next to a stump, log, rock, or similar shelter. The nest is just a scrape or hollow in the ground, which the female lines with grass or leaves. She usually lays 12 to 17 eggs, and incubates them for 21 to 23 days while the male stands watch.

The quail's young, like those of other ground-nesting birds, are on their feet shortly after their down dries. Chicks have been seen running from danger with eggshell still stuck to them. After just ten days, they can make short flights, and in two weeks they are accomplished fliers. The parents introduce their brood to things good to eat: primarily seeds, but also leafy plants, insects found on the ground, and berries. They also learn to pick up grit, which helps grind up food in their gizzards.

The family is large enough to form its own covey—and so it does, at least until fall, when families unite into larger groups. The covey roosts each night in a sheltered spot, generally in bushes or trees 15 to 25 feet above ground.

Quail may walk long distances in search of food, and when they find it, one of the males is posted as sentry. They tend to feed for an hour or two after sunrise and before sunset. Quail have also been known to frequent backyard bird feeders and birdbaths. Despite their dispersal in the spring, and occasional forays from their home range in search of food, California quail generally remain in the same territory of less than one hundred acres their entire lives. Their mountain quail relatives, by comparison, move up and down in elevation in response to the changing seasons.

Quail are beset by many enemies, approaching from land or air, including skunks, ground squirrels, foxes, raccoons, snakes, owls, hawks, and, of course, human hunters. Despite this, studies have shown that their life spans are surprisingly long in the wild—six-plus years. Which probably proves that if you are a bird that prefers to walk rather than fly, there is safety in numbers.

Mourning Dove

Latin name: *Zenaida macroura*

Description: 10 to 12 inches; tan overall, scattered black spots on back; long, pointed tail; wings make whistling note when bird flies.

Habitat: Suburbs, agricultural lands, woodlands.

Scientists now know that a lot of birds once thought to be monogamous (true to a single mate throughout their lives) have secret lovers on the side, or break up as soon as they have left their breeding territory. But even in this era of reduced avian family values, a mated pair of mourning doves remains true-blue for life.

Established pairs and younger, unattached birds gather in large flocks in winter (some mourning doves winter in the Northwest, while others go as far south as Panama). With the arrival of spring, the flock disperses. Bachelor males find a suitable territory and begin the plaintive, dawn-to-dusk *coo-cooing* that led people to tag this species the "mourning" dove. The female, who presumably finds the call more enticing than melancholy, flies in to inspect the singer. He launches into the air and comes down gliding and circling above her. On the ground, he struts about with bobbing head and spread wings. If she is convinced that he is her one and only, the two will mate.

Mourning doves are also paragons of domestic harmony in the way they share the chores of making the nest and raising their young. Over the course of one to three days, the male brings twigs and grasses to the female, who creates a flat and utterly flimsy nest with them. This is often positioned on the horizontal branch of an evergreen, but might be placed on top of another bird's abandoned nest.

After the female deposits her two eggs, the prospective parents take turns incubating them for the next two weeks; the male takes most of the day shift, and the female replaces him for the night. As they care for the eggs, both parents begin forming "pigeon's milk" in their crops. The crop, a saclike food storage chamber, allows doves (and their relatives) to take in large amounts of food, which can be digested later, when the bird is safely under cover. The pigeon's milk is a white, curdled substance secreted by the walls of the crop. Ninety-nine percent of the adult mourning dove's diet consists of seeds, but the young require protein and fat to develop properly. Many seed-eaters provide this by feeding insects to their young, but doves and their relatives rely on nutritious pigeon's milk.

The parents regurgitate the milk, and the young receive it by sticking their bills into their parent's throats. After five days, they are fed their first seeds, softened with the milk. Both parents produce the milk for at least another week, and the father continues to produce it for four to six days longer than the mother. When the young leave the nest, he also tends them while the mother prepares for her second brood. A pair typically produces at least two or three clutches. Mourning doves experience a high first-year mortality of 70 to 80 percent, mostly due to hunting. The species has expanded in numbers, however, because it responds well to many of the environmental changes brought about by encroaching human settlement. Doves can take advantage of the open areas and the weed seeds that spring up on farms, pastures, and fields; they also accept seed and corn from backyard ground feeders.

Human activities had the opposite effect on the doves' relative, the passenger pigeon. (The terms "dove" and "pigeon" are interchangeable; it's convention rather than scientific determination that gives these two birds different common names.) The passenger pigeon looked much like a larger mourning dove, minus the dove's characteristic black spot near the ear. Today the extinction of the passenger pigeon seems as ancient and inevitable as that of the dinosaurs. But a few generations ago, people marveled at the immense numbers of these birds. Credible estimates of flocks number in the billions. A part of my written family history includes this description of how my great-great-grandparents, sitting in front of their log cabin in Pennsylvania, "often saw great clouds of passenger pigeons":

> I say "clouds," for they covered the sky until the sun was sometimes darkened; thousands of them, tens of thousands, flying to and from their roosting places in the great woods. Market men with poles and nets and guns went to these great roosts where the limbs of the trees were often broken down by the tremendous flocks. They went by night with torches and gathered in these birds by the tons and shipped them in barrels to the cities.

The account adds that my great-great-grandfather "used to discuss the fate of these flocks which reached in a solid mass for miles upon miles. They are gone."

The mourning dove escaped the passenger pigeon's fate partly because it does not nest in the phenomenally large numbers that the pigeon required for its survival. The mourning dove remains our most widely distributed native dove—but the extinction of the passenger pigeon lessened our world in ways the current generation cannot fully realize.

Canada Geese

Latin name: *Branta canadensis*

Description: From 22 to 45 inches, depending on the species; black head and neck; broad white chin strap; brown back and wings; white belly; black bill, legs, and feet.

Habitat: Areas with or near water, including estuaries, marshes, mudflats, parks, shores of rivers, lakes, grasslands, meadows, and farm fields.

C anada geese know a good thing when they see it. And city parks, corporate business headquarters, and golf courses—with their inviting ponds and their nicely kept lawns—are good things to the honkers. As a result of this increase in habitat (among other factors), some races of Canada geese are experiencing a population explosion.

These best known and most readily recognized of all wild geese are so numerous in many areas of the country that they are considered a nuisance. It's surprising to learn, then, that the largest race was once feared to be extinct. In 1962 a population of giant Canada geese, found in Minnesota, relieved fears that this race had completely disappeared.

At least eleven races of honkers are recognized, from the small, almost mallard-sized "cackling" Canada goose up to the nearly swan-sized "giant" Canada goose. The races tend to remain distinct because they are loyal to their separate breeding grounds. The birds can be further divided into the semidomesticated residential geese of park and fairway, and the more wary and shy migrators, who winter in the Pacific Northwest but breed in the far North.

It is these clamoring wild birds that call our attention to the skies each spring and fall as they migrate in V-formations. Their resonant calls are believed to be one way the birds assure one another they are still together. One theory about those classic formations is that each bird (except the lead) receives lift from the wing-tip vortices of the bird ahead of it. This is such a tidy, intriguing theory it's a shame that reality doesn't seem to back it up. Motion pictures show that the birds do not tend to position themselves in such a way to take advantage of the theoretical lift. Another theory suggests that the birds spread out this way simply to minimize chance of collision and maintain visual contact. This theory is not nearly as tidy, but it might work for the birds.

Regardless of how they get to their breeding area, all Canada geese share certain traits. They form long-term pair bonds, perhaps mating for life. A courting male impresses his female by lowering his head to within an inch of the ground and hissing loudly. He shakes his feathers and may, in a grand finale, link his neck around hers. After the wooed female succumbs to his charms, she makes a nest, usually near water. She usually lays from four to seven eggs, which she incubates for the next month, while her mate stands guard, hissing at anything that wanders too close. The female leaves the nest twice each day to eat, preen, and otherwise take care of personal goose needs. Once the young are hatched, the family quits the nesting area within 24 hours. The male leads his family to the water, where the young quickly learn to dive to escape danger.

While they are teaching their offspring what to eat and how to avoid predators, the parents lose their flight feathers in their annual molt. By the time the adults are ready to fly again, their young are also ready to try their wings. If they are migrators, the family will join other families to make the long journey. The young remain with their parents for a surprisingly long time, even returning to the breeding grounds with them on the next spring migration. It will be another two years before the juveniles are ready to mate, but they finally leave their parents as that pair begins to raise another brood.

These migrating geese aren't the ones that tend to pose a problem to humans (in fact, in some areas, their numbers are declining). It is the resident populations, with their slimy droppings and aggressive nest defenses, that come into conflict with golfers, park-goers, homeowners, and business people. A lack of natural predators and an abundance of food result in lots of fat, happy geese and lots of disgruntled, messy-shoed people.

The conflict, especially acute in the Eastern and Midwestern states, is also building here in the Pacific Northwest. Some states have taken strong measures against the resident geese. Many now allow hunting during times of the year when the migrants are gone; golf courses are using border collies to herd the birds; residents are breaking or shaking eggs (the birds will continue to incubate shaken eggs, but will lay more to replace broken ones). In some areas, goose task forces also herd the molting (and therefore flightless) birds into pens. The birds are slaughtered and the meat given to charitable organizations.

But in the Northwest (except notably, in Seattle), the geese are more often tolerated—so far. In suitable habitats like golf courses, the Canada geese continue to play through.

Red-Tailed Hawk

Latin name: *Buteo jamaicensis*

Description: About 19 inches; variable coloration, generally brown above; white or buff breast, streaked with brown; rust-colored tail.

Habitat: Open landscapes for hunting and woodlands for nesting.

Look in any bird book published in the 1950s or '60s and you're likely to find a heartfelt defense of red-tailed hawks, a spirited denial of the false accusations against them as "chicken hawks," and a plea that farmers stop shooting them out of the sky. Recent books are more relaxed: laws now protect all predatory birds, and most farmers have gotten the message that red-tails feed primarily on rodents, not poultry.

The red-tail soaring above a farmer's field is searching for voles, mice, squirrels, gophers, rats, snakes, and even crickets, grasshoppers, and other large insects. These hawks also hunt in open woodlands, meadows, and grasslands. On sunny days, they often perch on fence posts, telephone poles, or light poles beside freeways to survey their territory for tasty tid-bits. If you're not in the habit of scanning the poles along highways as you drive, start glancing up: you may be surprised how often you'll spot a hawk, especially on sunny days.

Red-tails are the most common hawk seen in the Pacific Northwest—and across the rest of America. Their coloration varies but they tend to be darker in the West than in the eastern United States. Occasionally red-tails here are so dark they look almost black, and only the color of their tails give them away.

If you're trying to distinguish male from female, however, that chestnut-red tail won't help. The two sexes look the same, though the female tends to be larger. If you happen to see two adult red-tails tolerating each other's presence, you can assume they are a mated pair.

But if you spot two involved in aerial displays, it can be difficult to know whether they are a pair deciding to mate or a resident bird chasing away an intruder. The acrobatics look similar. Typically, one hawk will fly above the other, swooping down occasionally. The lower bird may meet these swoops by turning upside down and extending its talons. If the two birds (of either sex) are engaged in a territorial dispute, the resident bird will be the attacker, and the trespasser will likely be chased out of the area. But if they are a pair about to mate, the male will be the upper bird, the female the lower. They will eventually fly to a tree, where the male will mount the female.

The pair may remain together for years. If one dies, another hawk is likely to take both the territory and the surviving mate as a package deal. Both male and female red-tails build the nest, a bulky affair that requires a strong base. The nest is often in the crotch of a high tree, on a sturdy, thick limb, or on a cliff face. Sometimes an abandoned squirrel or owl's nest is used as a foundation and is improved upon. The nests are often used annually—and added to each time—so that they sometimes become a foot or more taller than the parent birds themselves.

Like some eagles and other hawks, red-tails have a habit of dropping fresh green sprigs of pine, cedar, or hemlock into their nests. Researchers have advanced various theories explaining this: the sprigs may add moisture, or provide a clean place for the young to stand in a soiled nest, or—perhaps most probable—they may exude chemicals that inhibit parasites.

The three to five eggs are incubated by both male and female, and the adults are liable to abandon their nest if disturbed. The eggs hatch after four or five weeks; the young are ready for their first flight six or seven weeks later. They usually land in nearby trees and may remain there a few days, screaming demands for food at their parents. As the young increase their flying skill, the parents respond less to their food requests.

The immatures lack the chestnut tail coloration of their parents, and they can be difficult to identify until their adult plumage grows in. Hawks in general can be difficult to distinguish from one another, so I find it very convenient that the Northwest's most common hawk has a conspicuous and identifying mark—the red tail for which it was named.

Northwestern Garter Snake

Latin name: *Thamnophis ordinoides*

Description: 24 inches long; background color black, dark brown, tan, gray, or olive green, sometimes bluish; often has three stripes, one down back and one on each side, but either back stripe or both side ones may be absent, faint, or interrupted; back stripe yellow, orange, red, white, or blue; side stripes usually yellow or white.

Habitat: Parks, gardens, forest edges and clearings, thickets, fields, meadows.

I was enjoying the sun on my face during an early spring walk when I became aware that I was not basking alone. A slight *ssss* of scales against the dried grass of the roadside drew my attention downward, where I saw a slender tail disappearing into the overgrown weeds. Now I watched the ground as I walked and was rewarded by the sight of more garter snakes basking at intervals among the weeds. When I passed a woman heading in the opposite direction, I almost greeted her with "Watch for snakes!" before I realized she might take that as a frightening warning instead of a friendly suggestion. I settled for a boring but non-threatening "Hello" instead.

So many people are afraid of snakes that it's been suggested this fear could be an inherited trait of our species. Or it might simply be a learned response, one that can be unlearned. Garter snakes would be a good place to start. They are slight, colorful, and harmless. Because they're active during the day, they are by far the most often encountered snakes in the Northwest, and of the various garter snakes found in the region, the most common is the northwestern garter snake.

This native snake doesn't hesitate to go out and about in the rain. A little precipitation doesn't stop it from taking care of business, such as hunting slugs and earthworms. The northwestern garter also occasionally eats insects, snails, frogs, fish, salamanders, and small mammals.

Among the many creatures who would make a meal out of *it* are hawks, owls, Steller's jays, herons, gulls, weasels, raccoons, mink, and foxes. The garter's defenses include letting loose musk and excrement from its anal vent (cloaca)—as anyone who has caught one is liable to attest. It's been suggested that the snake's widely variable coloring and patterning may make it more difficult for a predator to learn to recognize the species as prey. (Those colorful stripes are also how the garter snake got its name, back in the days when men wore striped garters to hold up their socks.)

Northwestern garter snakes hibernate during the winter months, often in communal groups tucked deep within rock crevices or talus slopes. After emerging in the spring, the female garters leave scent (pheromone) trails in their wakes. The males follow these paths with flickering tongues. The tips of a snake's forked tongue collect trace chemicals from the air. The tongue tips are then inserted into an organ on the roof of the mouth, allowing the snake to analyze and identify the taste/smell. You've probably seen an inquisitive snake flicking its tongue in and out trying to get some information about you; the male on the trail of a female does the same thing.

When he encounters her, he rubs his chin along the length of her back and tries to lie beside her. She requires some convincing, but eventually, after the male's repeated twisting and attempts at alignment, an acquiescent female opens her vent and allows him to insert one of his two hemipenes (twinned penises) into her cloaca. Her body will store his sperm until the eggs are ready for fertilization.

Rather than laying eggs, garter snakes retain the eggs within their bodies and give birth to live young. The average litter numbers six to eleven, usually born between July and October.

With the birth of her snakelets, the mother's duties are finished, and family members go their separate ways. Like other snakes, northwestern garters instinctively know how to hunt and hibernate. Like other Northwesterners, these snakes also know how to appreciate the spring sunshine.

Garden Slugs

Latin names: *Limax maximus* (great gray garden slug);
Arion ater (European black slug); *Deroceras reticulatum* (milky slug)

Description: To 5½ inches long, depending on species; four retractable
tentacles on head; saddlelike "mantle" caps front top of body; remainder of body
or "foot" can be characteristically smooth or furrowed, depending on species.

Habitat: Moist, dark hiding places during the day;
gardens, parks, cities, suburbs, country.

Picture this: You're in your backyard or garden, minding your own business, when you notice a blob that seems to be hanging in midair near a tree. Upon closer inspection, the apparition turns out to be two entwined slugs—great gray garden slugs, to be precise—that are suspended upside down from a branch by a cord of slime. From the impassioned manner in which the two are twisted around each other, you have a sneaking suspicion what they're up to. But by the time each extrudes a startlingly blue appendage from near its head, and these appendages also entwine and even change shape, you may be wondering just what is going on here: If these slugs are mating, which is male and which female?

Great gray garden slugs *are* able to copulate in a manner likely to impress even the most talented trapeze artist. And each partner is both male and female; slugs are hermaphrodites. The blue appendages (sometimes more of a milky color) are penile sacs, which exchange sperm. After completion of the act, the two will climb back up their slime line and part company. Eventually, each will find a nice moist spot to lay its eggs.

Depending on such factors as the air temperature and moisture, the eggs will hatch within eight weeks (those laid in fall will overwinter). The hatchlings that survive their perilous youth will quickly grow up to leave silvery trails on your sidewalk, patio, or deck on their leisurely way to chow down on your garden plants.

Just about any slug that attacks your garden plants is a non-native. Species indigenous to the Northwest, such as the large, usually yellowish banana slug (*Ariolimax columbianus*), prefer forested habitats and eschew cultivated landscapes. The introduced species rode in on plants and produce from Europe, Asia, and the Eastern United States, and found the moist conditions of the Pacific Northwest much to their liking. In addition to the great gray garden slug, two species you're apt to encounter are the European black slug and the milky slug (occasionally called the gray garden slug).

These three species can be readily distinguished from one another. The black slug grows the largest, at five and a half inches, and is indeed often black, or a dark reddish brown; the wrinkled and furrowed texture of the foot is characteristic. The great gray remains truer to the color of its name and grows to about four inches; look for a smooth, unwrinkled foot, and spots or streaks on its mantle. The milky slug, at about two inches long, is usually brownish or gray, with some mottling, and has a ridge that runs the length of its body; the mantle has visible concentric folds.

But perhaps you're more interested in how to kill slugs than how to identify them. Although slugs may be blamed more often than they deserve for damage to both ornamental and food plants, it is true that they are one of the major culprits. David George Gordon's *Field Guide to the Slug* describes several methods for killing them. Two of the most popular local ones are salt and beer. If the slugs had a vote in the matter of their own dispatching, they'd likely choose death by beer.

A shallow hole is dug and fitted with a tin pie pan, plastic butter tub, or similar container so that the container's rim sits at ground level. The beer poured into the container is sometimes made more enticing by adding a bit of baker's yeast. Overnight, the slugs will be lured by the siren smell of malt and yeast and, eventually, also by the drowned bodies of their fellow imbibers.

This frat-house–party method is less cruel than simply salting a slug, but not because the beer-swilling slugs are presumably too inebriated to care about their imminent demise. Gordon suggests that because a slug's body is covered with nerve endings, salting it causes it "undue pain." So if you feel you must go to war against your backyard slugs, consider their tender nerve endings. Kill the beasts with kindness by inviting them to drop in for a beer.

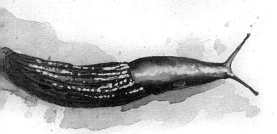

Praying Mantis

Latin name: *Mantis religiosa*

Description: 2 to 2¹⁄₂ inches long; green or tan overall; triangular head with two bulging eyes; long, slender body; first pair of legs usually held in folded position; each has a white spot with a black margin near where it attaches to body.

Habitat: Fields, gardens, meadows, thickets.

Kiki the praying mantis came to live with us for a few weeks one fall. Our cat first noticed the tan insect when it landed on the side of our house; I captured it before she could and placed it in the dry rock-and-twig-lined aquarium we keep ready for small unexpected guests. I wanted to observe the mantis for a time, but the eerie thing was that, with its big bulging eyes and swiveling head, the insect often observed *me*.

With the help of field guides I determined that our visitor was a European mantis. This species, accidentally introduced on nursery stock delivered to New York in 1899, is now one of the most common in the United States. I also decided that the mantis was probably male, judging by its slender abdomen at a time of year when females should be corpulent with eggs. Undeterred by scientific reasoning, my daughter Hallie decided his name was Kiki.

That first evening we noticed that Kiki's eyes changed color. Tan during the day, they turned black as evening approached. The darker pigment absorbs more light, allowing mantises to hunt at night as well as during the day. Three smaller eyes (often visible in close-up photos but not readily apparent in life) form a triangle between the insect's antennae. These probably register only light and dark, not the complex mosaic-type vision afforded by the two larger eyes.

We kept Kiki well supplied with crickets and grasshoppers, which he watched avidly and, when they blundered near, nabbed with startling speed. Mantises will also take on bees, beetles, caterpillars, butterflies, aphids, and other insects. Often they fastidiously clean themselves after a meal, delicately nibbling their legs and antennae and rubbing their heads with forearms, much like a cat. Although captive mantises can learn to sip water from a spoon or a drop on a finger, Kiki usually clung upside down from the screen covering the aquarium. So rather than risk the possibility of a flying escape into the house, we thought it better to spray droplets against the glass that he could later sip.

But because it was fall, I knew Kiki might be interested in matters beyond food and drink. We released him in the garden, wondering if he would eventually find a female to woo. Mantises do not survive the winter, but their walnut-sized egg cases do.

You've probably heard rumors about the bad manners of the female praying mantis during sexual relations. Since the late 1880s, various books, articles, and scientific papers have described the mating of mantises and its apparently inevitable cannibalistic conclusion.

In this translation from J. Henri Fabre's 1907 ten-volume opus, *Souvenirs Entomologiques,* the French entomologist describes the mating of two captive mantises and reveals his horrified fascination:

The male, absorbed in the performance of his vital functions, holds the female in a tight embrace. But the wretch has no head; he has no neck; he has hardly a body. The other, with her muzzle turned over her shoulder continues very placidly to gnaw what remains of the gentle swain. And, all the time, that masculine stump, holding on firmly, goes on with the business! . . . A headless creature, an insect amputated down to the middle of the chest, a very corpse persists in endeavoring to give life. It will not let go until the abdomen, the seat of the procreative organs, is attacked. Eating the lover after consummation of marriage, making a meal of the exhausted dwarf, henceforth good for nothing, can be understood, to some extent, in the insect world, which has no great scruples in matters of sentiment; but gobbling him up during the act goes beyond the wildest dreams of the most horrible imagination. I have seen it done with my own eyes and have not yet recovered from my astonishment.

More recently, researchers have suggested that such staged matings between captive mantises, though often repeated over the years with similar results, have resulted in a skewed view of the mantis's sex life. Newer experiments show that a more natural mantis encounter begins with a dance by the male to placate the robust female. She responds with ritualized movements of her own, which progress from a menacing stance to one of acquiescence. The male then climbs onto the female's back, deposits his sperm into a special chamber, and is allowed to leave with his head intact.

In these experiments, the researchers made sure that they themselves could not be seen by either participant (as Kiki proved, mantises are well aware of their keepers); past researchers may have affected the insects' responses simply by the act of observation. Another possible explanation for the aberrant mate-munching is that the gravid females were simply famished. Kiki averaged about four crickets a day; a female with eggs might require fifteen.

Thanks to this scientific update, we can be reasonably sure that Kiki did not suffer the same macabre fate as Fabre's male mantises. But the tale of the headless lover has been around for over one hundred years and is hard to get rid of. The Cannibalistic Praying Mantis Bride may be the first documented insect urban legend.

Grasshoppers

Latin name: Order Orthoptera; various genera and species

Description: To about 3 inches long; large eyes on sides of narrow head; antennae less than half of body length in short-horned, body-length or longer in long-horned; strong hind legs; hardened forewings come together in a peak over body and cover pleated hind wings when at rest.

Habitat: Fields, roadsides, lawns, woods.

Grasshoppers are the Jekyll and Hyde of the insect world. They are ordinarily considered cheerful chirpers who add a pleasant background buzz to summer and fall days. But given the right circumstances, including a high population and a scarcity of food, they turn into a plague of locusts that strip huge areas of all vegetation. Many people probably consider the grasshopper an entirely different animal from the locust of biblical and historical records, but science recognizes them as one and the same: cicadas are also sometimes called locusts.

Which is not to say that *all* grasshoppers are capable of darkening the skies with their numbers. Some species are simply more destructive than others. For example, the Carolina grasshopper (*Dissosteira carolina,* also called the Carolina locust), which is found in the Pacific Northwest and throughout most of the rest of the United States, isn't usually considered a pest. This is the familiar grasshopper we see in dry lawns and fields and along dirt roads, which rises into the air with a whirring of dark wings bordered with pale yellow. (The closely related long-winged locust [*D. longipennis*] *is* quite destructive but, happily, is not found in the Northwest.)

Grasshoppers are divided into two groups according to the length of their antennae. Short-horned grasshoppers are those whose antennae are one half or less of their overall length. These include the locusts and are the creature most people picture when they hear the word "grasshopper." Long-horned grasshoppers have antennae that are body-length or longer, and are actually more closely related to the katydids and even to crickets than to the short-horned grasshoppers.

By midsummer or fall, both groups are singing, but they produce their music in different ways. Long-horneds rub their wings together like crickets; short-horneds rub the spurs of their hind legs over a scraper on their wings, making a buzzing sound, like running a fingernail over the teeth of a comb. Long-horneds, again like crickets, "listen" to the songs of their species by picking up vibrations with membranes located on their legs. Short-horneds listen with similar membranes on their abdomens.

Regardless of how their music-making and listening are accomplished, these behaviors serve one purpose: reproduction. Males fiddle to attract females; females listen to locate males. Long-horneds tend to mate at night, with those extravagant antennae helping to direct the operation. Shameless short-horneds mate on your lawn in broad daylight.

The short-horned mother-to-be is quite particular, however, about where she will lay her eggs. She repeatedly probes the ground with an egg-laying organ at the rear of her abdomen called the ovipositor. Scientists think she actually tests the soil for such things as soil temperature, water content, acidity, and salt levels. When satisfied, she uses her ovipositor to burrow into the ground, creating a narrow tunnel in which to lay her eggs. She then covers them with a sticky solution that dries and hardens into a durable, waterproof shell.

The eggs overwinter, but their parents do not survive the cold weather. Come spring, the little hoppers emerge from their underground natal chamber, looking like tiny, pale versions of the adults. They spend the spring and summer eating the plants their species prefer, molting several times as they grow. In addition to their prodigious hopping skill, they deter their many enemies by spitting an acrid, brown substance often called "tobacco juice." At their final molt, they achieve adulthood and, for the first time, full wings. And with those wings, they gain not only the ability to fly, but the ability to make music. By midsummer or fall, grasshoppers are in fine fiddle.

Western Thatching Ant

Latin name: *Formica obscuripes*

Description: About ¼ to ⅜ inch long; head and thorax reddish, abdomen and legs black.

Habitat: Forest edges and meadows.

I once spent a day helping my entomologist friends Jim McIver and Torgy Torgersen measure an ant nest. This feat required a crew of people and took several hours because it was no ordinary ant nest, but a "super colony" of the western thatching ant. Jim and Torgy's final calculations suggested the colony's two hundred and ten interconnected nests covered ten acres and housed fifty-six million individuals.

Jim later calculated that the super colony would annually consume the equivalent of sixteen thousand quarter-pound hamburgers. Of course, ants usually consume their protein in the form of insects, not McDonald's burgers. And super colonies are a rare occurrence. You're far more likely to see single colonies of these ants, which might house a hundred thousand individuals (and annually consume the equivalent of thirty quarter-pound burgers).

Thatching ants are easily identified by their distinctive home: a mound that may stand one or two feet high. In the Northwest, a nest is composed of sticks, and its "thatch" covering is mostly dead fir and pine needles.

Pheromone (scent) trails radiate away from the mound like highways. During the warm months, these trails teem with busy workers, all of whom are nonreproductive females. According to their size, large and small workers assume different duties. Each small worker travels a particular highway that leads her to a plant that hosts aphids. Her main duty is to tend this group of aphids her entire working life, protecting them from predators and gathering "honeydew" from them. Honeydew consists of droplets of excreted sugars, which the ant solicits by stroking the aphids with her antennae. A small ant spends her one year of life hustling back to the colony with this bounty and then returning for more.

The larger workers' careers are more diversified; they will perform three tasks in their two-year lifetimes. After pupation from larvae into young adults, they remain inside the nest and become living pantries for the colony. Their voracious appetites allow them to consume relatively large amounts of insects and honeydew brought to them by older workers. Their abdomens, oily with the protein-rich food, swell to three times their normal size. Through regurgitation, the young adults will feed the entire colony throughout the winter months.

With the coming of spring, these ants graduate from food-storage units to the second phase of their lives, maintenance workers. Now they patrol the top of the nest, keeping it in good repair. As they pass into the final stage of their lives, the large workers become scavengers. Each regularly canvasses a specific area, collecting dead or dying insects and delivering them to the nest. When the arrival of cold weather curtails their activities, they will retire into the nest to spend a second winter. Come spring, they will once again be valuable to the colony: they will live only a few more months, but that will be long enough for them to reestablish the previous summer's trails.

Because thatching ants are so adept at storing food, they are able to raise a reproductive generation even before foraging begins in spring. The queen, safely ensconced in the depths of the nest, lays eggs that will hatch into males and reproductive females called queens. In April or May, the reproductive winged individuals rise up out of their nests and mingle with the males and queens of nearby colonies.

Mated males don't live long, but a mated female goes on to establish her own colony and may live twenty-five years. She has two methods of finding her new home. Because she is unable to create a new colony by herself (unlike queens of most other ant species), both methods involve finding an established colony. When she finds one containing her own species, she quickly sheds her wings and absconds with a number of workers, who simply walk off the job and follow her to a new site. This method, called "budding," can be compared to the swarming of bees that establishes a new hive.

In the second method, the queen lands on the nest of a related species of ant, *F. fusca*. She goes down into the hole, finds the reigning queen, and kills her. The *F. fusca* workers will now raise the alien queen's offspring, which will gradually usurp the original occupants as they die off. This murderous method of colony establishment is probably the more common of the two.

It's still not understood why some of these nests will stand alone, their residents ready to wage war against other thatching-ant nests that intrude on their territory, while another nest might develop into hundreds of interspersed, interconnected mounds, like the one Jim and Torgy discovered. But whether they live in a small mound or a massive super colony, thatching ants form a complex society of workers and warriors, all of whom retain fierce fealty to their clan and queen.

Ladybugs

Latin name: Family Coccinellidae; several genera and species
Description: Red or orange with black dots, or black with red or yellow dots.
Habitat: Gardens, backyards, farms, fields; an introduced species may overwinter in houses (also under bark, logs, and in crevices outdoors).

When is a bug not a bug? When, like a ladybug, it has jaws. Entomologists will tell you that among other distinguishing attributes, true bugs are jawless and have a sucking mouthpiece like a sharp, hollow bill. The ladybug is a beetle, and for that reason purists sometimes call it the "ladybird beetle."

Nor is a ladybug necessarily female. Males and females look alike to us, but their common name doesn't refer to gender. According to folklore, in the Middle Ages the farmers of a certain village prayed to the Virgin Mary when aphids were destroying their grape vines. The round red insects showed up in huge numbers to devour the aphids and were dubbed "ladybugs" in gratitude to "Our Lady."

Ladybugs are still welcomed in gardens and on farms today for the same reason. They are easily the most beneficial of all our insects because they prey on mites, insect eggs and larvae, and aphids—especially aphids. (Unlike ladybugs, aphids *are* true bugs. These tiny, plump insects have a tubelike mouthpiece that they insert into plants to suck out the juices.) It has even been reported that ladybugs are unable to reproduce unless they have eaten aphids.

Armed with this knowledge, I gathered the neighborhood kids one summer afternoon for a foray into a nearby field to hunt ladybugs. We quickly captured several, and after adding a few plant stalks loaded with aphids (which were, of course, the reason why the ladybugs were in that field in the first place), I became a ladybug rancher for about a week. The first evening a pair mated, and a day later I noticed a cluster of tiny yellow oval eggs on the underside of a leaf. These hatched after about five days into a horde of minute gray larvae that looked like elongated triangles dotted with bristly black warts. The young have been described as looking more like alligators than ladybugs.

The larvae are voracious aphid eaters and are sometimes called "aphid wolves." Concerned that I wouldn't be able to supply enough food for the large brood, I soon released them onto the artichokes in my backyard garden, which had an infestation of aphids.

The larvae go through three molts, splitting their old skins and changing color as they grow. After about two weeks, they attach themselves to the bottom of a leaf and hang motionless. The skin splits one last time to reveal a plump, round pupa with markings similar to the red or orange and black markings we associate with adults.

During our foray in the field, the children and I had had the good fortune to find one of these pupas and had placed it, with its leaf, in a second jar. I checked it daily, but by the time I'd freed the larvae the pupa still had not changed. I'd nearly given up hope that it was still alive when its skin split down the back and a fresh new ladybug emerged. It was initially a pale orange with no markings, but after some hours, its shell, or outer wings, had hardened and turned black with two orange dots. I freed it on the backyard roses, which had their own profusion of aphids.

Ladybugs come in red, orange, or black, like my newly hatched ladybug.

larva

Some have no spots, while others are decorated with two to fifteen. What appears to be the shell are really two outer wings that cover and protect the two used for flying. Ladybugs lift these two outer wings and unfold the long inner ones when they want to get somewhere fast.

As with other brightly colored animals, the ladybug's conspicuousness serves as a warning. Birds reportedly don't like its taste. To further discourage predators, the ladybug can play dead, rolling on its back with legs folded. A truly aggrieved ladybug will exude sticky and foul-tasting yellow fluid from its leg joints.

Despite these defense mechanisms and its voracious appetite for defenseless aphids, the ladybug seems like a genteel sort of beetle. It is not only the most beneficial, it's also easily the most beloved of all our insects. It makes no difference to the ladybug's good reputation that its name is entirely deceptive. Not only is it not a bug, the "lady" may even be a he.

Western Tent Caterpillar

Latin name: *Malacosoma californicum*

Description: Up to 2 inches long; body orangish brown with
blue markings, covered with long hairs.

Habitat: Silken tent in crotch of broadleaf tree, frequently red alder,
during the spring and early summer months.

Many caterpillars, such as the tiger swallowtail caterpillar, are known by the name of their adult stage. But it's not uncommon for species that are considered pests to be named after their larvae. The mature form of the tent caterpillar, for example, is so short-lived and inconspicuous compared to its obnoxious larvae that *it* is named after *them.* The tent caterpillar moth might live only one day—just long enough to mate and leave the eggs that will produce the next generation.

The female lays those eggs in a single cluster of a few hundred on a twig of red alder or another species her young will find delectable when they emerge. The inch-long egg case will overwinter, protected by a shiny, dark, water-resistant coating. Lengthening days and warming sun will lure out the tree's buds and new leaves, along with the hungry caterpillars that will eat them.

Soon after they emerge, the larvae begin to spin a sheltering tent, typically in a fork of the tree's branches. Working with its siblings, a caterpillar discharges silk from a spinneret on the bottom of its head. Together they wrap sheetlike webbing around the tree branches. Like the caterpillars who weave it, the nest starts out small. As the larvae molt and grow, they add additional layers of webbing. Each layer has air space that separates it from the previous one, allowing the caterpillars to crawl around inside. Older, inner layers contain the insects' feces and old molted skins.

The caterpillars must regularly leave their tent, usually en masse, to forage. Each larva lays down a silken trail as it ventures out, as well as a pheromone (scent) that will help it find its way home again. Sometimes the brood defoliates its natal tree, and individuals must strike out to find new feeding areas. If one finds an appropriate spot, it eats its fill. When the sated caterpillar returns to the tent, its siblings can recognize from its pheromone trail that it has found food, and follow the trail back to the new territory.

Tent caterpillar population outbreaks are cyclical, and in some years it seems as if nearly every red alder in the land is covered with the creepy-crawlies. (These infestations are often said to occur every ten years, but the timing is actually more irregular than that.) My husband and I vividly recall walking down a tree-lined street one sunny day in Olympia, Washington. Instead of being in robust leaf, the alders looked dismal: each was blanketed with silken tents, and many of the branches looked skeletal. In the midst of our conversation, we suddenly became aware of a low-key but clearly audible background sound. The realization struck us simultaneously: we were hearing the *munch munch munch* of millions of caterpillar mouthparts—accented, perhaps, by the faint sound of their feces hitting the pavement. We suddenly felt like characters in a low-grade Hitchcock movie.

Even when it seems that tent caterpillars are taking over the world, predators are stepping in to save the day. Birds, viruses, and even annoyed homeowners armed with tree clippers and matches take their toll. Tachinid flies (which resemble large houseflies) lay eggs just behind the caterpillars' heads, where they cannot be chewed off. This white spot, which is clearly visible, marks the caterpillar's doom. When the egg hatches, its larva burrows into the caterpillar and feasts on it from the inside. Although tent caterpillars recognize the buzz of the fly and thrash their upper bodies about in an attempt to ward off her parasitic attack, plenty of the flies find their mark.

The relatively few caterpillars who survive the onslaught will find a protected place to spin a cocoon. About two weeks later, a nondescript adult moth (beige with two dark bands on the wings) will emerge and go in search of a mate. Males trace the sex pheromones released by females, who are usually mated within hours of leaving their cocoons. The adults don't even have functioning mouthparts: they simply propagate and die.

Because tent caterpillar moths accomplish their mission by midsummer, they can't be blamed for the tree-tents we see in the autumn. Those are made by fall webworms (*Hyphantria cunea*), which get a later start in the year because they overwinter as cocoons, not eggs. Their adults (a type of tiger moth) are emerging from their cocoons when tent caterpillars are emerging from their eggs. In addition to the difference in timing of web construction, the fall webworm weaves its home in a tree's branch tips, not in its forks. It also includes food leaves in its nest, so it doesn't have to leave the shelter to eat.

Fall webworms begin making their webs soon after tent caterpillars finish—a sort of horror-movie sequel—but the two kinds of tent-builders are not closely related. Despite their similarities, the lives of fall webworms and western tent caterpillars follow different plotlines.

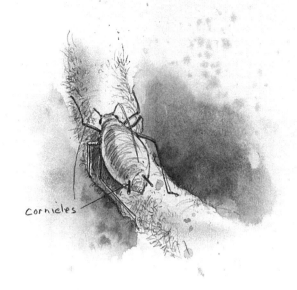

cornicles

$\frac{1}{16} - \frac{3}{8}''$
actual size

Aphids

Latin name: Family Aphididae; various genera and species

Description: ¹⁄₁₆ to ³⁄₈ inch; plump bodies, tiny heads, long antennae; may be green, red, black, or brown, with or without wings.

Habitat: Fields, croplands, orchards, gardens, weedy areas.

Aphids manage to crank out generation after generation without bothering to mate . . . or lay eggs . . . or even stop eating. Like some other insects, aphids reproduce by parthenogenesis, a term that translates as "virgin birth."

The first generation of each year erupts in spring. Having spent the winter in eggs their mother conveniently laid on their food plant, the emerging young are all females—every last one. Each promptly sticks her beaklike mouthparts into the growing portion of her host plant. The sisters feed voraciously, molting as they rapidly outgrow their own skins. At maturity, without benefit of mating, they produce a second generation—again, all females. Because their eggs mature inside them, these subsequent generations actually give birth to live young. An aphid may birth a dozen or so babies within twenty-four hours, popping them out her back end, without so much as withdrawing her beak for a glance in their direction. This new generation also soon gives birth to females.

And so it continues into the summer, until the host plant becomes overcrowded or begins to die. At this point, some of the most recent generation develop into winged adults—although, again, all are female. They use their feeble little wings to carry them to another plant. Some of the winged aphids might get a free ride on air currents to a new place miles from their original home. When they land on appropriate host plants, these pioneers begin new all-female wingless colonies.

Depending on the species, as many as thirteen generations may be produced by the end of the summer. The males finally make their debut in the last generation, which also includes females. In some species, the males are born without mouthparts and never eat. They have one single, important job: to stir up the stagnating gene pool and keep it healthy. They mate with the females who will lay the eggs that overwinter to create the next year's first generation of flightless, parthenogenetic females.

The rapid-fire, ferocious fecundity of aphids is the best defense afforded the fat little plant-suckers. By season's end a single aphid would be the matriarch of many billions—if she and her offspring were not such incredibly easy pickings, especially for lacewings and ladybugs.

Some aphids have another defensive trick up their cornicles, however. Cornicles are a pair of thin tubes that extend from the rear of the abdomens of most aphid species. In some, these tubes can secrete a waxy material that is pushed into the face of an advancing predator. By the time the indisposed attacker has cleaned off the yellowish, rapidly drying gunk, its intended victim may have shifted out of reach. But a far more effective defense of aphid colonies is made by their benevolent caretakers, the ants.

Ants and aphids form a symbiotic relationship—that is, one in which both parties benefit from the association. The ants protects the aphids and in return they receive honeydew from the aphids. An aphid tapped into the sappy juices of a plant takes in more sugar than it can use, so it excretes sweet droplets called honeydew. If there are no ants around, these drops will fall on leaves, where they are eaten by butterflies, bees, and flies. (Or, if the aphids are in a tree, their tiny taffy-drops may be cleaned off by aggrieved car owners who think the tree itself is somehow responsible.) But with ants to attend them, the aphids hold in the sugary liquid until an ant solicits it by stroking an aphid with its antennae. The aphid responds with a larger droplet than it would otherwise produce, and the ant has a feast. Ants go to great lengths to protect their miniature cows. Some species even take aphid eggs into their nests below ground for the winter, then deliver the hatched newborns to their appropriate host plant in the spring.

The aphid's meager talents are not appreciated by farmers, orchardists, and gardeners, however, some of whom call the little insects "plant lice." One tiny guzzler on her own would make not a whit of difference, but taken together, plant lice are mighty Amazons capable of wreaking havoc. Aphids stand united, shoulder to shoulder in sisterly, plant-sucking, baby-spewing solidarity.

Woolly Bear Caterpillar

Latin name: *Pyrrharctia isabella* (formerly *Isia isabella*)

Description: To 2 inches long; body completely covered with dense hairs; reddish brown or orange-brown band of varying width around middle; black at both ends; black head.

Habitat: Meadows, fields, roadsides, pathways, leaf litter.

Why does the woolly bear caterpillar cross the road? In the autumn it wanders far and wide in search of a cozy, safe place to spend the winter, so we're more likely to notice it on roads, sidewalks, or trails than in the surrounding vegetation. Most moth and butterfly species overwinter tucked into protective eggs or in sturdy cocoonlike pupae, but the woolly bear remains in its furry larval stage. Once it finds a suitable place—under the bark of a tree, under a rock, or in duff and leaf debris, the woolly bear simply curls up for the duration.

The real riddle might be: What does a woolly bear eventually turn into? Answer: After pupation in the spring, it emerges as the lyrically named Isabella tiger moth. There are a number of different kinds of tiger moths, and most have bold stripes on their wings, but the Isabella sports only small black spots on its yellowish or orangish wings. Although it is a good-sized moth, with a wingspan of up to two inches, we are not as familiar with it as we are with its larval stage because, like most moths, it is nocturnal.

After mating, the females lay their eggs in clusters on various plants their offspring will eat. After just four or five days, the eggs hatch and the young begin feeding. The larvae go through several molts as they grow into the familiar woolly bear caterpillar. This summer generation doesn't have to be as finicky about finding a place to pupate as its overwintering parents were, which may be why we don't see as many of its members roaming about.

Having found a protected spot, the woolly bear spins a cocoon out of silk and hairs from its own body. After two weeks, the adult Isabella tiger moth breaks free of its enclosure and flies off in search of a mate. It is the offspring of this generation that we'll notice in September and October.

The woolly bear might be childhood's favorite caterpillar. Even as adults, many of us harbor a soft spot for the fuzzy-wuzzy things that curl up in the palms of our hands. (A few people develop a rash or some other allergic reaction after handling woolly bears. Those hairs come off easily and can irritate, so it's a good idea to wash your hands well after holding one.) The caterpillar's tendency to ball up when disturbed is a protective maneuver: few predators relish hairy entrees. Skunks, however, roll the caterpillars on the ground to wear off the hairs and then gobble the denuded result.

Folklore suggests that the width of the rusty band on woolly bears predicts the coming winter's weather. A wide band is said to mean a mild winter, while a narrow band suggests colder than normal temperatures. But what the orange belt truly reveals is the age of the woolly bear; it grows wider as the caterpillar matures. (There is, however, great individual variation; some larvae simply have wider bands than others, regardless of age.) Perhaps the legend resulted because people noticed that in the years when winter got an early start, the woolly bears seeking shelter had narrow bands—because the caterpillars were younger when winter arrived. Even though they can't really forecast the weather, woolly bear caterpillars that take to the road are a sure sign that winter is not too far behind.

ADULT

Earthworm

Latin name: *Lumbricus terrestris*

Description: To 11 inches long; slender body, segmented except for a smooth encircling band.

Habitat: Almost anywhere with soil and green plants.

Earthworms are not only underground—they're underrated. These lowly animals perform valuable services for which they are rarely given credit. While going about their daily lives, earthworms not only turn over soil, aerating and loosening it, they also eat up dead things and poop out fertilizer.

No less eminent a naturalist than Charles Darwin spent forty years studying earthworms and wrote an entire book about them. He recognized the impact they have on soil, pointing out that earthworms tilled the earth long before the plow was invented. Darwin estimated that each year the earthworms on one acre bring fifteen tons of soil to the surface.

All of this means nothing to the earthworm, of course. It's just trying to eat, reproduce, and avoid becoming someone else's lunch. Because it is a tasty morsel enjoyed by so many animals, the earthworm tends to be a homebody, rarely leaving its burrow. It ventures out at night, usually exposing only the top portion of its body, which probes the area around its burrow, seeking food or a mate. Delectable meals to an earthworm are dead leaves or decaying plant or animal material; a desirable mate is likely to be the worm next door. Earthworms prefer the security of having their hind ends in their burrows while they mate. Nor is the gender of the worm next door a problem—every earthworm has both male and female sex organs.

Mating worms position themselves belly to belly with their heads point-ing in opposite directions. Each has an encircling smooth band, called a clitellum, which now exudes a sticky mucus that binds the worms together, and the two exchange sperm. Sex for these hermaphrodites is more com-plicated than a simple transference of sperm to egg, however. Fertilization does not take place immediately; instead, the sperm collected by each worm is held in a special pocket away from the eggs.

Some days later, the eggs within each worm mature. Its clitellum now swells and secretes a mucus ring that encircles the worm like a girdle. By contracting its muscles, the earthworm gradually moves the girdle over its front end, collecting the ripe eggs and waiting sperm along the way. When the mucus cylinder has been pushed entirely off the worm, its two ends seal. As the cocoon gradually hardens underground, fertilization finally occurs. The young worms crawl from the capsule after developing into miniature versions of their parents.

Earthworms are a basic and important part of the food web. Legions of animals feast on them, including birds, skunks, centipedes, shrews, lizards, gophers and moles—especially moles, which can eat their own weight in earthworms every twenty-four hours. Moles are even known to hoard earthworms in their underground burrows after first biting off their front ends to incapacitate them.

It is not true that a worm cut in half will generate new ends, resulting in two whole worms. Experiments have shown that they can regenerate a cer-tain number of segments from either end, but if a garden spade (or a mole) cuts beyond that limit, the earthworm is doomed.

Earthworms move through soil with the help of tiny bristles called *setae*. Each segment of a worm has four setae, which can be extended and retracted to help it move. The setae can also maintain a surprisingly fierce grip on the burrow—which you will have noticed if you've ever tried to pull a worm from its hole or watched a robin struggling for its meal.

If the soil is loose, earthworms dig by pushing the particles aside, but if the soil is compacted the animal simply eats its way through. Its crop (similar to that of a chicken) contains tiny bits of rock that grind the soil, and its digestive system extracts minerals and organic matter before the worm excretes the remains. The waste of worms, called castings, consists of humus and nutrients needed for plant growth.

It's easy to take earthworms for granted, but Aristotle called them "intestines of the earth," and Darwin doubted there were any other animals "which have played such an important part in the history of the world."

Mourning Cloak Butterfly

Latin name: *Nymphalis antiopa*

Description: To 3⅜ inches wingtip to wingtip; wings deep purplish brown with bright blue spots outlined by pale yellow; black undersides of wings blend with dark tree bark.

Habitat: Open woods, meadows, fields, parks.

Mourning cloaks, like many butterflies, are solar powered. Because they can't generate their own body heat, mourning cloaks depend on the sun's rays to warm them—which explains why you won't see them on dark, overcast days.

But you might see a mourning cloak on a sunny day in the middle of winter or on those very first gloriously bright spring days. Most butterfly species spend the winter as eggs, caterpillars, or chrysalises, but the mourning cloak overwinters as an adult. It survives the cold weather tucked behind a tree's loose bark or wedged in some other crevice, so it's one of the first butterflies to greet spring.

In light of this, the mourning cloak would seem to deserve an optimistic and heartening common name, but apparently its somber coloration impressed people more. That dark color, a rich purple-brown of the wings, no doubt allows the insect to absorb more warmth from the sun's spring rays.

Mourning cloaks put in such an early appearance that none of the fruits they will be drawn to later in the summer are available. Instead they rely on sweet sap that oozes from broken twigs and branches. Their adult status means that mourning cloaks get a head start on the business of mating and egg-laying.

Courtship consists of brief chases and might include a short spiraling dance that carries the pair upward into the air. Occasionally you may see two of these apparently infatuated butterflies spiraling twenty to fifty feet in the air before one suddenly plummets to earth and the other slowly meanders back down. It's speculated that, in such cases, the male has found a female who has already mated (and is likely in the process of laying her many eggs). She initiates the spiral and he follows—up to a point. Apparently recognizing that the relationship is going nowhere fast, he abruptly gives up the chase. Her slower return trip may give him time to become intrigued elsewhere.

When the gravid mother lays her eggs, she chooses plants her young will eat upon hatching, recognizing their preferred willows, elms, or cottonwoods with hairlike taste receptors on her feet. Most butterflies lay single eggs, but the mourning cloak deposits hers in clusters, the minute eggs nestled together on a twig or surrounding it like a tiny pearl-studded collar. Before they hatch, the eggs will darken to nearly black.

Once liberated, the tiny caterpillars set to work chewing on the food plant their mother chose for them. Because they tend to stay together, the larvae can be tough on trees. Elm trees have been so defoliated that the mourning cloak young are sometimes called "spiny elm caterpillars." If disturbed, the siblings' response is to twitch or shake in unison, which may be disconcerting enough that a predator will leave them alone.

After four molts, they reach their full size of about two inches, and by this time the family has likely broken into smaller groups. Now each surviving sibling finds a secluded spot where it can attach itself for a final molt. This time the shucking of the skin reveals a chrysalis. Over the following two weeks, the caterpillar's tissues and organs are literally dissolved and rearranged into those of a butterfly.

The emerging mourning cloak expands its damp, folded wings by pumping blood into them before it can fly off to feed and mate. In contrast to the handsome top surface of its open wings, when it's at rest the stippled undersides of its closed wings camouflage it against dark tree bark. If disturbed, the insect launches into flight, producing a "click" that is apparently used to startle potential predators.

That click, the mourning cloak's gregarious young, and its early-spring appearance all diverge from the usual butterfly habits. Although it is quite common and is found throughout much of the Northern Hemisphere, the mourning cloak is truly one of a kind.

Daddy Longlegs

Latin name: *Phalangium opilio*

Description: Oval body, surrounded by and suspended from eight long, slender legs; brown or gray. (Note: A similar-looking spider lives inside houses, but it has a segmented body and spins a web.)

Habitat: Gardens, lawns, fields, woodpiles.

The one thing you may think you know about daddy longlegs is not true. They are *not* spiders. Daddy longlegs and spiders are both arachnids, but they differ from each other in several ways. Spiders have eight eyes and two distinct body sections, while daddy longlegs have only two eyes and an oval body in which the two sections are fused. Spiders are also able to generate both silk, with which to spin webs, and poison, with which to paralyze their prey; daddy longlegs can generate neither.

Longlegs do, however, have scent glands on either side of their bodies that can release an acrid odor when they are attacked. The smell has been likened to that of rancid nuts. Their two eyes are located on a tiny turret toward the front of their bodies, each permanently looking sideways.

But daddy longlegs are best known for their eight fabulously long and fragile-looking legs,

which they use for more than just walking. The legs contain sensory equipment, and the second pair—the longest ones—are the most sensitive. When trying to determine what is happening around them, daddy longlegs will lift this pair and wave them furiously in the air. They occasionally lose their legs from mishaps or in close escapes from predators (the twitching severed leg may distract the attacker while the animal makes its getaway). Unless it loses one of the second pair, this does not seem to hamper a longlegs. If it loses both of the second pair, it reportedly will die.

Longlegs amble about, seeking soft-bodied insects such as aphids, or perhaps some plant material for lunch. When they find food, they seize it with two small appendages at the front of their bodies and pass it to their slender jaws, or *chelicerae.*

On their walkabouts, daddy longlegs are also looking for mates. They mate frequently, indiscriminately, and without much ceremony, though they may touch one another with their legs. The opening for their reproductive organs is located near the front of the body, on the underside. Unlike other arachnids, daddy longlegs have organs that allow direct copulation. A bigger surprise than learning that longlegs are not spiders might be that the males have penises. Two mating longlegs face one another and the male extends a long penis and inserts it between the female's chelicerae and into the oviduct.

Shortly after mating, the female searches for an appropriate place to lay her eggs. She requires a moist substrate—perhaps some moss, rotten wood, or damp soil under a stone. Once she has found it, she extends an impressively long tube, or ovipositor, and thrusts it into the nesting material to deposit her eggs. They number in the hundreds, and she will lay several broods in her yearlong lifetime. Once the eggs are laid, the ovipositor telescopes back into her body and her motherly duties are completed. The eggs will overwinter if it is late in the season. But if the ground is still warm, the young will hatch and creep out. They grow slowly, molting eight or nine times and changing from white to the brown or gray coloration of adults.

Although adults are around in early summer, they are especially noticeable in fall, and for this reason daddy longlegs are also called harvestmen. Large groups of them sometimes congregate in some warm or sunny spot, standing with their legs comradely intermingled. Since spiders tend to be solitary creatures, even in this habit daddy longlegs show their difference from the cousins they so resemble.

Black~and~Yellow Garden Spider

Latin name: *Argiope aurantia*

Description: Up to 1⅛ inches; black and bright yellow (or orange) markings on body; dark legs held in X formation.

Habitat: Gardens, backyards, meadows, fields, especially in sunny spots.

*f*ew creatures have as accurate and descriptive a common name as the black-and-yellow garden spider. Even if you've never heard the name before, you can probably immediately picture the species. This spider is one of the Northern Hemisphere's most common, while its habit of sitting smack dab in the middle of its web in the garden makes it obvious, and its large size and handsome yellow and black markings make it particularly eye-catching.

You're more apt to notice the larger female spider than the male. She spins the good-sized orb web (the classic type with lines radiating outward from a center hub and a connecting spiral over all) that the male visits in order to mate with her. Before going courting, the male has to prepare for the eventual sexual encounter. Like other spiders, he spins a small pad called a sperm web and squirts a dollop of sperm into it. He then soaks up the sperm with his two palps (short for "pedipalps"). These extend from the head and are also used to detect scents and vibrations. (By looking at a spider's palps you can recognize whether it is male or female: the male's palps look swollen while the female's are slender.) Each of the male's palps has an inflatable structure that works something like an eyedropper to suck up the sperm from the small web. When his preparations are completed, the male is ready to meet his mate.

A female orb weaver releases a pheromone (scent) that helps attract males of her own species to her web. Upon arrival, the male spins a mating thread, which he plucks in such a way as to entice the female and convince her that he is not food. Copulation is swift and consists of the male inserting his palps into the female's genital opening, located on the underside of her abdomen. The male will then probably set off in search of another alluring whiff of pheromone.

The female garden spider subsequently lays a spherical egg case, up to one inch in diameter, and dies shortly thereafter. Her babies hatch in autumn but remain inside the tough, brownish case, where the bigger ones survive the winter by eating the smaller. In spring the surviving spiderlings leave the case, each spinning a line of silk that catches in the breeze to lift and carry it away. They will molt several times before reaching the size of their parents.

The web of a black-and-yellow garden spider usually includes a white zigzag pattern, the purpose of which has engendered much speculation over the years. The conspicuous line is called a *stabilimentum* because it was initially assumed to stabilize the web. When tests proved that wasn't its purpose after all, other theories were offered. One proposed that the zigzag alerted birds to the web's presence so that they would avoid flying into and destroying it. Others suggested they were molting platforms, or that they helped conceal or disguise the spider hanging head down in the center of her web.

More recently, it's been shown that the stabilimentum is a spider's trick to lure flying insects into her web. Insects that pollinate plants are able to see in the ultraviolet light range (unlike humans), and the zigzags reflect ultraviolet light. The glowing patterns mimic the ultraviolet markings on flower petals that guide insects to nectar (rather like landing lights along an airport runway). Scientists used to think that spiders' webs were like sieves, passively collecting insects that happened to blunder into them; now it is recognized that the garden spider's web actually attracts her prey.

When the ruse succeeds, the struggles of the entangled insect signal "You've got food" to the spider waiting in the center of her web site. She moves quickly to wrap her prey in silk, and she might also immobilize it with a paralyzing bite. If she isn't particularly hungry, she will move the bundle to a more convenient place on the web. When she is ready for her entree, she injects the hapless victim with a digestive fluid and then slurps up a meal of liquefied insect.

This arachnid (spiders are not insects; one difference is that they have eight legs and insects have six) is sometimes called the black and yellow arigope, after its Latin name. Because of the stabilimentum, it has also been called the writing spider—and it is probably the heroine of E. B. White's *Charlotte's Web*. But instead of writing "SOME PIG!" as Charlotte did to save her porcine friend's life, the black-and-yellow garden spider's web is more likely to hail passing insects with the message "SOME FOOD!"

Meadow Spittlebug

Latin name: *Philaenus spumarius*

Description: Nymph: ⅛ inch; wedge-shaped, soft-bodied, yellow to pale green.
Adult: ¼ inch; oval, brownish body with spots; wings concealed unless in flight.

Habitat: On meadow and field plants, hidden within masses of froth.

Spittlebugs hide right out in the open. Despite their conspicuousness, few people seek them out because to do so means digging through a slippery substance that looks entirely too much like spit.

In spring and summer little white globs of spittle appear on plant stems, especially in fields and meadows. People I led on nature walks frequently spotted them and asked me what made the spit. Some assumed it had been left by a passing animal. Others had heard the foam referred to as "cuckoo spit," which confused them even more. I took a perverse delight in the grimaces and horrified looks of my guests as I gently sorted through the froth to reveal the tiny creature inside.

Spittlebugs are small and wedge-shaped, usually a pale green. They are the nymphs of froghopper insects. After they hatch in spring, the nymphs promptly insert their beaklike mouthparts into their host plant and start sucking. The plant's juices are all the nymph needs to sustain itself—actually, more than it needs; the nymph excretes the excess fluid, mixing it with a glandular secretion that stabilizes the resulting froth. A pumplike structure beneath the nymph's abdomen blows air into the liquid, creating bubbles one at a time and all the same size. The nymph invariably positions itself head downward so that the foaming mass cascades over its body.

As it sucks up the plant's juices, the nymph pumps away furiously, reportedly circulating one hundred and fifty to three hundred times its own weight every twenty-four hours. It needs a foam home to protect its soft body from predators. The mass also creates a constantly moist and cool environment that keeps the nymph from drying out. There is often more than one nymph inside each mass of froth, and a severe infestation can damage their plant host, stunting its growth 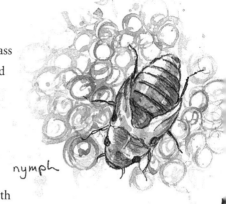 nymph and causing it to wilt. There are different species of spittlebugs, and they can be found on more than four hundred plants, including crops such as wheat, oats, corn, and strawberries. Clover and alfalfa are particular favorites of the meadow spittlebug.

The nymphs undergo several molts inside the spittle, eventually emerging as winged adult froghoppers, about one-eighth to one-half inch long and oval. Froghoppers are rather inconspicuous insects, similar in appearance to leafhoppers, and are brown, gray, or green, depending on their species. (The adult of the meadow spittlebug is brownish, spotted, and about one-quarter inch long.) Although the adults still eat the same types of plant juices, they give up their pumping and foaming habit and can now hop from plant to plant.

Froghoppers produce only one generation per year, laying their egg masses in late August or early September. Female froghoppers deposit up to thirty tiny white eggs in the crannies between the stems and leaves of succulent plants. The eggs in each mass lie neatly side by side, glued together with a frothy cement. The adults do not survive the cold weather, but the eggs overwinter and hatch the following spring. The nymphs seek a sheltered, humid area of the plant, point themselves downward, stick in their beaks and start pumping away.

For creatures that hide, spittlebugs certainly are conspicuous in fields in the summer. By gently probing into one of their globs of spit, you can reveal the little insects inside and amaze—or appall—your friends.

Yellow Jackets

Latin name: *Vespula* spp.

Description: $\frac{1}{2}$ to $\frac{5}{8}$ inch long; entire body boldly marked with yellow and black (white and black in some species); four wings, but hind ones transparent and difficult to see.

Habitat: Open areas, forests, meadows, fields, wetlands.

My friend Esther, a wetland biologist, had the misfortune to kick open a yellow jacket nest while doing a plant inventory. As she bolted to her car, she was stung many times. Shaken and upset, Esther did what any Pacific Northwesterner would: she drove directly to a coffee shop and ordered a latte. (When I suggested that a visit to a doctor might have been more appropriate, she exclaimed, "Hey! After that horrible experience, I *needed* a latte!")

To add insult to Esther's injuries, the yellow jackets that stung her didn't even have the decency to die afterward. Honeybees and bumblebees die after stinging because they become eviscerated. The bee's stinger is barbed, so it usually remains lodged in the victim's flesh when the insect flies away. Its venom sac, attached to the stinger and pulled out of the bee's body, continues to pump in venom even as the bee begins to die. Yellow jackets, however, have smooth stingers that can be repeatedly reinserted. The incensed insects live to sting again.

This is because bees use their stingers only as defensive weapons, while most yellow jacket species also use theirs to paralyze prey. Although the adults eat only sweet things like flower nectar, fruit, or tree sap, their larvae siblings back home require protein, so the adults kill caterpillars, aphids, and other insects, which they serve pre-chewed to the larvae. The grublike larvae reciprocate by feeding the adults a sweet substance.

A colony gets its start in the spring, when an overwintering queen emerges from beneath leaf litter. Having already mated the previous autumn, she becomes the founding mother of a bustling metropolis that at its peak may number five thousand individuals. After finding a suitable location for her new home, usually an abandoned underground animal burrow or occasionally an attic or crawl space, the queen creates a golfball-sized nest by chewing decaying wood or leaves into a gray papery substance. (Another type of wasp, misleadingly called a hornet, makes similar paper nests above ground, especially in trees and in house eaves.) The queen makes cells that receive her first eggs. After the larvae hatch, she tends and feeds them. Upon pupation, these larvae become the first workers, all of which are sterile and female. The sisters take over chores such as expanding the nest and perhaps the hole it is situated in, and feeding new larvae.

By summer's end, a relatively few fertile individuals, including some males, begin to be produced. These will carry on the colony's legacy; all its other members will die when cold weather comes. The males and the new queens leave the nest and likely mingle with reproductive members of other nearby nests. The males die after mating, while the females await the coming of spring under leaf litter. As the weather cools, the underground nests of the old colonies are likely to be dug up by skunks, raccoons, and other mammals who relish the protein-rich bodies of the now cold, lethargic residents.

Because the colony offers such a food bonanza, yellow jackets are defensive, even aggressive, during their warm-months heyday. Adding to their petulance is the conundrum that, as the summer progresses and the colony reaches its largest size, insect prey becomes harder to find. At this point the yellow jackets begin to rely more on scavenging than on hunting. By late August, the unruly, greedy and uninvited guests are showing up at just about every outdoor birthday party, picnic, and barbecue. The yellow jackets still want meats and sweets; they'll steal bits of hamburger or chicken in place of caterpillars, and sips of cola instead of flower nectar.

It's best to retreat slowly and steadily from a yellow jacket's unwanted attention. The party-crashers can turn nasty if swatted. When a wasp is injured or when it is stinging, it releases an alarm pheromone (scent) that is like a distress signal to other workers. It leads them to the aggrieved sister and they mount a vicious attack. Should you, like my friend Esther, find yourself at the receiving end of their wrath, run indoors or jump into water. It's also good to remember that people *can* outrun yellow jacket pursuers.

If you do get stung, apply meat tenderizer, an insect sting relief wipe, or a cool baking soda poultice to the stings. Multiple stings, however, should prompt an immediate call to your doctor, even if you're not usually allergic. And after *that*, you can get a well-deserved latte.

European ground beetle

Ground Beetles

Latin names: *Carabus nemoralis* (European ground beetle);
Pterostichus spp. (common black ground beetle)

Description: ½ to 1 inch long, depending on species; quick-moving, dark beetles
with long legs, narrow heads, large eyes and jaws.

Habitat: On ground in gardens, yards, open woods, sometimes farm fields;
often under logs, stones, etc. during the day.

*T*he Searchers may sound like the title of a movie coming soon to a cinema near you, but it actually refers to a type of ground beetle in a yard near you. The lifestyles of these arthropods would fit nicely into a low-budget thriller, however. A plot synopsis could read: *The searchers typically wait until dark to emerge from their dank hiding places. In black armor, they prowl the night with two intentions: to kill and devour their defenseless, soft-bodied victims—and to produce more of their own kind, who will also have but two desires. . . .*

But rather than making millions on the silver screen, ground beetles make an honest living in the garden. And gardeners can be glad they do, since those soft-bodied victims of the European ground beetle include slugs. As its name implies, this type of ground beetle was introduced from Europe (as were the non-native garden slugs it searches out). It also preys on cutworms and housefly maggots, and its control of these pests certainly outweighs the loss of the earthworms that it also takes. Now one of our most numerous ground beetle species, it prefers cultivated yards and gardens, though it also ventures into adjacent low-elevation forests.

The European ground beetle is, at first glance, similar to the various native Northwest species. These latter are usually lumped together under the descriptive—if not terribly imaginative—name of common black ground beetle. A quick check of the abdomen (and these beetles scrabble across the ground quickly enough that all you might get is a quick look) can determine which kind you've found. The European species has three rows of tiny pits along each of its two hard wing covers; the common black sports lengthwise grooves. In the right light, the European species glows an iridescent purple or greenish bronze. It also grows up to one inch long, compared with the common's largest length of five-eighths of an inch.

If cornered or sufficiently aggrieved, both kinds can emit a stinky liquid. The obnoxious odor is said to vary somewhat from species to species, but it is often described as somewhat vinegary.

Although the larvae don't have this same defense, they are also pugnacious, carnivorous hunters. Like the adults they will become, the young have prominent jaws used for tearing apart their prey. They eat the same types of food they will enjoy as adults, including caterpillars and other insects. The larvae begin as single eggs laid in the soil, in mud, or in duff and debris, depending on species. They hatch into hard-bodied, black elongated larvae and may remain in that larval stage for as long as two years before pupating and turning into adults. The adults of some species may then live for two years as well.

The Pacific Northwest boasts a number of different species of these insects (there are over three thousand in the whole of North America), and it can be tricky to tell them apart. But you don't need to be an entomologist to identify these beetles. Virtually any fast-moving black beetle you find on the ground can—conveniently and correctly—be called a ground beetle.

actual size

common black ground beetle

Mosquito

Latin name: *Culex pipiens*

Description: ⅛ to ¼ inch; two-winged, slender body. While feeding, holds its abdomen parallel to the victim's skin and its last two legs up at an angle.

Habitat: Ubiquitous; especially found near water.

A mosquito's main source of food is not human or animal blood, as you might reasonably suppose. In fact, male mosquitoes *never* take a blood meal and are content to sip flower nectar, fruit, and the sugary fluids of plants. Even the female gets most of her energy this way. The only time she seeks you out is when she needs protein to produce eggs.

The fact that a mama mosquito wants your blood not for her own meal but for the sake of her young is cold comfort when she's whining persistently around your head. That tormenting high-pitched drone of her wings is an alluring love song to a male mosquito. Different species have different pitches; a male recognizes his own species by the pitch of her wingbeats. Male mosquitoes have many fine hairs on their antennae, which resonate in response to the appropriate pitch. (Amorous males can also be attracted by the hum of electric wires and tuning forks.)

Once he has found a bona fide female, the male strokes her body with his legs. Taste receptors on his legs detect pheromones and confirm that she is the correct species. Males of several species pass a pheromone along with their sperm, which inhibits the female's desire to mate again. Instead, she develops blood lust. A mosquito can produce eggs without a blood meal, but this takes a terrific toll on her. Without protein from an outside source, she's forced to digest her own wing muscles, which permanently grounds her and also produces far fewer eggs. No wonder she's so persistent in her pursuit of blood.

Humans are not necessarily her first target. A mosquito takes blood from many other creatures, including birds, snakes, frogs, and nonhuman mammals. But mosquitoes are definitely more attracted to some people than to others. Sensors in the mosquito's front legs help her detect heat, and people differ widely in the amount of heat radiated by their skin. Mosquitoes are also attracted to the carbon dioxide released when we breathe (which explains why they tend to buzz around our heads) and which our skin also exudes. Other blood-sucking insects are drawn the same way, so if, like me, you're one of those people mosquitoes favor, then fleas and other bloodletters probably also find you particularly delectable.

The mosquito doesn't so much *bite* us as siphon or suck our blood. Her mouthparts have often been compared to surgical instruments. She first probes the skin with palps located on either side of her lower lip. Once she has located a soft spot or perhaps a pore, she sets down her lower lip, uncovering six tools needed for the operation. Four of these are needles that quickly pierce and slice through the skin. The remaining two tools are tubes, which are inserted into the incision; one sucks up blood, while the other injects saliva to prevent it from clotting. (It's the saliva that causes later itching and swelling.) The blood goes directly into the mosquito's gut, which expands mightily. She is capable of sucking in a blood meal heavier than her own weight. This makes her slightly sluggish on takeoff, however, upping our chances of swatting her.

The sated female flies off to find a place to lay her eggs, and in the Pacific Northwest she doesn't have to look far to find water. She doesn't require a whole pond—a puddle or a rain-filled hollow stump will do. The female lays one hundred to three hundred eggs in a cluster that stands on the surface of the water. The tapered tops and wider bases of the eggs cause them to lean toward the center of the cluster, stabilizing it.

When a larva is ready, it pops off the bottom of its egg and enters the water. It hangs, head downward, just below the surface, breathing through a snorkel-like tube near its tail. After a week or more, the larva becomes a pupa, and finally molts into its adult form at the water's surface. It emerges, dry, on top of the water and uses its own old skin as a launch pad.

Mosquito larvae in the water are eaten by water beetles, toads, turtles, and small fish like minnows. During their brief two- to three-week life span as adults they are especially sought by bats, dragonflies, swallows, and purple martins, as well as many other insects, amphibians, fish, birds, and mammals. Without these allies, many more mosquitoes would be making a meal out of you.

Bumblebees

Latin name: *Bombus* spp.

Description: Largest (queens) to about ⁷⁄₈ inch; covered with dense fur; black with yellow.

Habitat: Gardens, meadows, fields, marshes, woodlands.

lthough the female bumblebee comes equipped with a stinger, she is so mild-mannered, plump, and fuzzy that she could be considered the teddy bear of bees. Almost any bumblebee (or honeybee, for that matter) you're liable to encounter is a female. Certainly all of the ones seen in early spring are. These bumbles, which are larger and seem buzzier than those you'll see later in the summer, are mated queens that have spent the winter buried beneath fallen leaves. Barring mishap, each will become the matriarch of an entire colony of workers.

Because we usually see only a single bumblebee at a time, it's easy to assume that they are solitary creatures. But like the honeybee—whose habits are better known—a bumblebee comes from a large family and has a family home. Members of the queen's old colony died with the coming of winter, and one of her first royal duties is to establish a new home. She searches out the abandoned burrow of a mouse or other rodent and lines it with dried grasses, leaves, or moss. She'll often add more material to the burrow's opening, perhaps to camouflage it, because other queens who discover the home are liable to challenge her for it. Parasite bumblebees (*Psithyrus* spp.) also specifically seek out a *Bombus* nest to kill or subordinate the true queen and take over her family. (The family members end up tending the parasite's young, and eventually die without a succeeding *Bombus* generation to replace them.)

When she's satisfied with her cozy, insulated nest, the queen secretes wax from glands on her abdomen and fashions it into small cups called "honey pots." After visiting early-blooming wildflowers or trees, she regurgitates their collected nectar into the pots. In one pot she places pollen she has combed off her fur using her feet. To this pot the bee adds her first eggs, usually eight or so. She seals the pot with wax and then presses her abdomen against the pot to brood her eggs like an old hen. She works her muscles to create body heat and takes sips from the close-by honey pots to regain energy.

As her larvae hatch and grow over the next twelve days or so, the queen occasionally opens the wax seal to give them additional pollen mixed with honey. When they reach full size, the larvae spin silk cocoons, from which they will emerge as sterile female adults ten to fourteen days later. The wet and bedraggled sisters rest and feed from the honey pots for a couple of days, but then they have work to do. Their mother is already incubating more eggs, and it is now up to the workers to forage for pollen and nectar. As the colony grows, the younger workers will tend and feed the larvae while the older ones forage. The queen continues to lay and brood more eggs. At its largest, her family may consist of two or three hundred individuals.

Although bumblebees make honey, they manufacture only enough to feed the colony during the warmer months. They don't need to stockpile extra because, unlike honeybees, the entire colony will not live through the winter. As summer wanes, the queen begins to produce fertile offspring. Up until now, to each egg she laid she has added a sperm from a special sac that has held them since she mated the previous fall. Now she withholds sperm from some of the eggs, and these hatch into male bees (drones), which have no stingers and do no work for the colony. They have only one job to perform before their deaths: at maturity, the drones leave home and set up territories, which they patrol while awaiting the arrival of virgin queens. The drones leave pheromones (scent) on leaves and twigs to advertise their availability.

Larvae that are simply given extra food for a longer period of time develop into queens. At maturity these, too, disperse in search of males. A new queen may mate with several males before heartily gorging herself on the last of the season's nectar. With the arrival of cold weather, she buries herself beneath leaf litter to await the spring. When it comes, the bumble-bee will noisily extricate herself from the duff and trundle off to begin raising a whole big batch of daughters and a few sons.

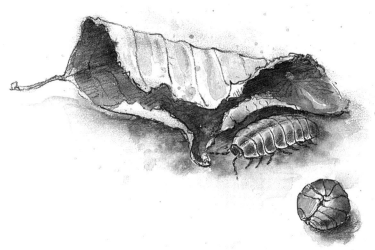

actual
size

Pillbugs and Sowbugs

Latin names: *Armadillidium vulgare* (Northwest's most common pillbug);
Porcellio scaber and *Oniscus asellus* (Northwest's two most common sowbugs)

Description: Less than ¾ inch long; oval, segmented body;
adults have seven pairs of legs.

Habitat: Moist dark places, especially under stones, rotting logs, leaf debris, woodpiles.

Because of the way they curl up into tight balls, pillbugs remind me of tiny armadillos. But they're also similar to two other (very different) animals: lobsters and kangaroos.

Their connection to lobsters is a matter of family ties. Despite their common name, pillbugs are not really bugs. Count their legs and you'll find fourteen—insects have six. Pillbugs and their close relations, sowbugs (the two groups are known collectively as woodlice and by the common names of roly-polys and potato bugs), are crustaceans, and they are more closely related to lobsters, crabs, and crayfish than to insects. The vast majority of crustaceans live in the oceans; woodlice are rare exceptions that have moved to land. But their gill-like breathing apparatus still requires moisture, so that's why you're likely to find them in damp places.

Sowbugs can be distinguished from pillbugs because they can't roll up in a ball, and because they have two small appendages (called uropods) extending from their hind ends, which pillbugs lack. But both kinds of woodlice are reminiscent of kangaroos, koalas, and opossums because they have special pouches to hold their young.

To begin the mating process, an amorous male woodlouse may wave his antennae at a female. If she's receptive to his attentions, he will climb onto her and lick her head and drum on her back with his legs for a few minutes. Dispensing with further foreplay, he shifts to a diagonal position across her back to access one of the two genital openings on either side of her body. After depositing sperm, he'll switch positions to the other side and repeat the process.

The female can store the sperm and may be able to produce two broods without a second mating. She develops a brood pouch on the underside of her body between the second and fifth pairs of legs, where the eggs are held for the next month or so. A watery fluid in the pouch bathes the eggs, which generally number a couple of dozen. When they are ready, the young, looking like white, miniature versions of the adult, crawl out of the pouch. Initially they have only six pairs of legs, but with their first molt they gain the last pair.

Woodlice continue to molt throughout their lives (and the larger a female gets, the more young she can produce—one pillbug reportedly had a brood of two hundred and sixty-seven young). When insects molt, their old exoskeleton splits down the back and they step out of it with a fresh new covering intact. Woodlice, however, molt in two parts, over a period of a few days. A woodlouse's skin splits around its middle and it sheds the back half first. A day or so later, the skin again splits around the middle, and the woodlouse loses the front half. The animal often eats its shed skin, apparently to recycle the calcium it contains. In fact, people once ate woodlice as a cure for upset stomachs, and it's speculated that the calcium carbonate in the little crustaceans' exoskeletons neutralized stomach acids.

A molting woodlouse tends to hide because its soft shell makes it especially vulnerable to predators, including shrews, birds, newts, frogs, toads, and small mammals. The woodlouse itself is a scavenger that eats mostly vegetation. It transforms decaying matter such as dead leaves and rotting wood into minute waste particles that enrich the soil.

A sowbug, amazingly, can drink water from either end—with its mouthparts or by using the uropods on its posterior. The uropods can be held together to form a tubelike structure, which the sowbug presses against a moist surface. Capillary action draws the water up and into the anus.

Although they evolved from sea creatures, woodlice can tolerate only so much moisture. If they get too waterlogged, they are attracted to light and seek drier habitats. By pressing against a dry surface, a sowbug can also use its uropods to release excess water—again, by capillary action.

But most of the time you'll find sowbugs and pillbugs in dark, damp places. The next time you see a pillbug curl into a ball, maybe it will remind you of a lobster, a kangaroo, and an armadillo all rolled into one.

Crane flies

Latin name: *Tipula* spp.

Description: Gray or brown body ³⁄₈ to 2½ inches long, wingspan to 3 inches; wings largely clear but may be patterned; six long, slender legs.

Habitat: Moist, shady places, moss, mud, gardens, woodlands, near streams and lakes.

C rane flies are often subject to two opposing cases of mistaken identity. Some people are convinced they're giant mosquitoes, while others call them "skeeter-eaters." I was squarely in the latter camp for years, but for the record, crane flies aren't mosquitoes, nor do they eat them.

In fact, most species of crane flies, as adults, don't eat anything at all. They just seem to cruise around, dragging those long legs behind them. They often bumble into houses, apparently drawn by the lights. Although this sometimes seems to me like their life's ambition, judging by the number that manage to find their way into my house in fall, what they're truly interested in at this stage of their lives is reproduction.

In spring and fall, great mingling swarms of the things can be found in damp and

halteres

watery places. Some species choose a particular tree or bush to gyrate over. Bobbing up and down as if in anticipation, shifting and weaving, the males "dance" as they await the arrival of a female. When one appears, she is quickly seized by one of the dancers, and the two land somewhere to mate, tail to tail.

The females of some species may lay their eggs in shallow water, but most crane flies deposit their eggs in moist earth. These hatch into larvae known by the biker-club-sounding name of leatherjackets (gained by virtue of their tough outer coating), which feed on decaying vegetation in the soil, sometimes terrorizing suburban lawn-owners. After a few weeks, the leatherjackets pupate, transforming themselves into flying adults. Crane flies produce one or two generations a year, and most species over-winter as pupae.

Like all true flies, crane flies have one pair of normal wings, plus a second pair that have been reduced to knobbed projections called *halteres*. These are balancing organs that keep the insect on an even course. As it flies, the halteres vibrate, going up as the wings move down and down as the wings move up. If even one haltere is lost, the fly can no longer navigate. Because crane flies are so large and because they often remain still as we approach, they give us the opportunity to see halteres that are too small to notice on houseflies and mosquitoes. The next time a crane fly stumbles into your house, look for the twin projections that look like slender ball-headed pins, located just behind the wings.

A crane fly's great gangly legs are easily detached, which helps get the insect out of spider webs and other sticky situations. Those loose limbs also led to the folkloric belief that when a cow or some other item of property was lost, a leg pulled off a crane fly would help find it: the leg would gradually straighten out and would supposedly point in the direction of the lost creature. I'd be happy, though, if only those stiltlike legs could help show the crane fly the way out of my house.

field Cricket

Latin name: *Gryllus assimilis*

Description: To about 1 inch long; black or dark brown overall;
two long antennae extend from head, two shorter antennae extend from abdomen;
females have an ovipositor between the shorter antennae.

Habitat: Fields or around houses.

Crickets sing with their wings and listen with their legs. Their chirping calls are one of the expected backyard noises of midsummer and fall. We don't hear them in the spring because the young, which overwintered as eggs in the ground, don't yet have wings. These nymphs are in the process of molting and becoming adults.

Like other insects, crickets have no bones. Instead they have a hard exterior shell called an exoskeleton. When they are young, the exoskeleton eventually becomes too small for the growing animal, so the cricket molts. Its back splits open and the nymph wiggles free, its new, soft exoskeleton already in place. The new exoskeleton soon hardens and, in time, must be shed again. The cricket molts eight to twelve times, gaining its wings the final time. If it is a female, she also develops an ovipositor (egg-laying organ), which looks like a long, sword-shaped tail.

The ovipositor is the key to identifying a cricket as a female. Otherwise, the two sexes look very similar. Both are black or dark brown, with long antennae in front. Sticking out from the back end of their abdomens are two shorter antennae called *cerci*. The cerci help the animals maneuver in the dark and guide them when they are backing up, like metal "cat whiskers" on cars. The female's long ovipositor is situated between the two cerci.

Crickets have two sets of wings, one thin pair pleated underneath a leathery set. The wings lie flat against the back. (This is one way to tell crickets from grasshoppers, which have wings that come together over the back like a peaked roof.) Instead of using their wings to fly, crickets walk where they want to go, or depend on their strong hind legs to leap away from danger. Only the male appears to use his wings, and when he does, flight is the furthest thing from his mind.

He raises the two tough outer wings at a forty-five-degree angle and saws one of them against the other. Although both wings have the appropriate apparatus for making sound, most crickets are right-winged—that is, the right wing passes over the left. A series of ridges on a wing vein rub against a hardened section of the other wing's edge to produce the male's steady *breep-breep* song. The space between the raised wings and the body acts as a kind of echo chamber that helps amplify the sound.

The male cricket is not a traveling troubadour. Instead, he has a little burrow in the ground and sits singing in front of it, apparently optimistic that a female will track him down. She does this by walking around, moving her legs to determine which direction the song is coming from. Near the knees on each of her front legs are ears: tiny oval membranes tightly stretched like the skin on a drum. She's interested in only one song, the one unique to her species. (Like birds, cricket species can be identified by their calls.)

After the female finds the male, he woos her with a softer "courtship song." When they finally mate, he attaches a tiny packet of sperm to her abdomen. Sometimes she is more interested in dinner than in reproduction and eats the packet before it can fertilize her. But if fertilization is successful, within a few days she pierces the ground with her ovipositor and lays one hundred and fifty to four hundred tiny eggs, one at a time. There may be fifty or more within a two-inch-square area. The eggs laid in late summer and early autumn will hatch the following spring and will be responsible for the next season's serenade. On warm evenings when you hear a male cricket singing with his wings, chances are there's a female cricket out there somewhere, listening with her legs.

European Earwig

Latin name: *Forficula auricularia*

Description: ½ to 1 inch; dark brown, slender body; pincerlike appendages on rear of abdomen.

Habitat: Dark, constricted recesses during the day such as under stones or boards, or in woodpiles or plant leaves.

Earwigs may be little, but they look as though they mean business. They are the insects with pincers at the back end that you're likely to find under rocks or tucked into tight petals and leaves in your garden plants.

There are various theories about what those pincers, or forceps, are used for. But the most obvious reason is also the most plausible: earwigs use their forceps mostly for defense. If you've ever disturbed an earwig, you've probably seen it raise its abdomen menacingly. It has also been suggested (and refuted) that earwigs use their pincers to capture small insects, or to help them fold their long, delicate inner wings and tuck them in behind the harder protective pair of modified wings on their backs. (Not all earwig species have wings, and not all those who have them can fly. The delicate wings are not usually visible—they are folded both crosswise and lengthwise in order to fit beneath the shortened outer ones.)

It's also been reported that males use their forceps to battle sexual rivals. Despite the fierceness of the weapons, however, neither insect gets hurt; the stronger simply asserts his dominance by pushing the weaker one out of the way. One thing that *is* certain about the European earwig's forceps is that those of males are more curved than those of females, so you can use them to determine an individual's sex.

Folktales once claimed that earwigs crept into the ears of sleeping people, where—depending on which superstition you reference—they would either bore into the person's eardrum or burrow into the brain, causing insanity or death. Perhaps people believed the superstitions because earwigs like to inhabit narrow spaces. Cramming its body into a tight place triggers a resting response in the insect. Earwigs also tend to move upward, against gravity. Gardeners who want to rid their plants of this insect take advantage of these two tendencies by hanging up hollow plant stems, pieces of old garden hose, or rolled-up newspapers. The earwigs climb up into these narrow spaces during the night, and the gardener disposes of them the next morning.

But this doesn't seem worth the trouble unless the insects become destructive. Earwigs are usually a minor pest, although they do eat some plant material (they especially seem to like dahlias and hollyhocks). Because they forage at night, you are unlikely to see them during the day unless you disturb their hiding place. Likely places to find earwigs are in cracks, crevices, under bark, beneath stones and boards—anywhere tight and dark.

You're less likely to find their eggs, which are laid underground. After mating, the female digs a little burrow and then guards the eggs for two to three weeks until they hatch. For an insect, she is an unusually attentive mother. She regularly turns and cleans the eggs. And if her young are threatened, she'll defend them with opened pincers, or pick them up in her mouth and move them. She continues to guard her babies after they hatch, bringing food and frantically gathering them if they disperse. However, they are strongly motivated to leave after a week or two, when she develops a tendency to eat them.

Their lifestyle must serve them well, since the fossil record shows that earwigs have been around for at least one hundred and eighty million years. These hardy insects shared the earth with the dinosaurs—but they didn't do so in what's now the United States. The oh-so-common earwigs are non-natives, inadvertently transported throughout the world in plant material from Europe. The Pacific Northwest has the distinction of being the first place in the United States where earwigs were recognized—they were first reported near Portland, Oregon, in 1909. Since then, European earwigs have wasted no time in making themselves at home throughout the Northwest.

Dandelion

Latin name: *Taraxacum officinale*
Description: Bright yellow flower head to about 2 inches wide; flexible hollow stalk can rise to over 2 feet tall; rosette of ground-hugging, toothed leaves.
Habitat: Fields, lawns, woods, roadsides, sidewalk cracks.

It takes years for kids to lose their love of dandelions. Most of us once gathered the sunny blooms by the fistful and presented them proudly to our mothers. We also scrambled to collect the fluffy seed heads for the thrill of launching their parachutes into the air. But sooner or later we were told that blowing on the seed heads spread more dandelions, which was bad because they were weeds. It wasn't much of a leap after that to realize that dandelion flowers were not really appropriate bouquet material.

Still, not everyone grows up to disparage dandelions. Plenty of people look forward to the plants' first springtime leaves for use in a salad; later they may also harvest and eat the flowerheads and roots. Dandelions are an especially nutritious vegetable. The leaves have more iron, calcium, and magnesium than spinach or broccoli. The plant is also rich in beta-carotene, potassium, lecithin, phosphorus, and vitamins A and C, as well as a long list of other trace vitamins and minerals. Stories are handed down through families of how the nutritional power of dandelions supplemented meager Depression-era meals, or helped keep alive relatives who were in concentration camps or prisoner-of-war camps.

American colonists thought so highly of the dandelion as an herb and a vegetable that they carried it with them from Europe to cultivate in their new home. (The dandelion may have already beaten them here, having wafted over as seeds from Asia.) Of course, the colonists didn't have big swaths of lawn in front of their cabins to fuss over. When Americans later decided to surround their homes with a monoculture of cultivated grass, the assertive dandelion was demoted from a favored herb to an obnoxious weed.

Dandelions have now traveled, or been introduced, all over the world, and they are arguably the planet's most successful weed. Several factors give them advantages over other plants, including their reproductive strategies. If you think dandelions multiply so quickly in your yard that they must be cloning themselves, you're right: the plant can reproduce regardless of whether its flowers have been pollinated. The female parts of the plant can produce a viable seed without the benefit of the pollen manufactured by the male parts. It is thought that most dandelions begin this way.

Genetic diversity is introduced when a flower *is* pollinated by a bee, wasp, butterfly, beetle, or fly. What appears to be the flower of each plant is actually a grouping of one hundred and fifty to two hundred tiny, individual flowers called florets. Each has its own pistil and stamens, and each will form its own parachuted seed. Until that occurs, the green bracts close up around the florets to protect them at night or whenever it rains. The bracts also close while the florets produce their seeds, opening for the last time when the seeds are ready to be launched.

The wispy parachutes of the seeds, called pappuses, fan out into the familiar "blowball." The fine hairs of the pappuses come together in wet weather, but on dry, sunny days they spread out, ready to hitchhike on a breeze. Dandelion seeds can stay aloft as long as the relative humidity is less than seventy percent. When the humidity rises, as it does before a rain, the silky hairs close up, and the dandelion seed comes down, plants itself on earth—and gets watered.

The dandelion has other slick survival tactics. As almost everyone with a lawn can attest, the plant can regrow from just a portion of its taproot, which can go two or three feet deep to reach extra water and nutrients. The dandelion's hollow stalk can remain low to the ground or, if surrounded by high-rise plants, stretch up a couple of feet to lift its flower head into the sunshine. The flexible stalk bends with the wind, and grows higher when the pappuses are ready to ride the wind. And the dandelion discourages other plants from growing too closely: its rosette of leaves exudes an ethylene gas that discourages competition.

The jagged pattern of those leaves inspired the French to name it *dent de lion* ("tooth of the lion"), which eventually morphed into our "dandelion." France is one of many countries that still considers dandelions to be vegetables and sells them in its markets. They are also sold in some American supermarkets, and there are dandelion recipes galore available on the Internet, in books about wild foods, and even in specialized dandelion cookbooks. So, if you're tired of weeding them, consider eating them.

Blackberries

Latin names: *Rubus ursinus* (Pacific blackberry, trailing blackberry); *R. discolor* or *R. procerus* or *R. armeniacus* (Himalayan blackberry); *R. laciniatus* (evergreen blackberry)

Description: Slender, thorned shoots (canes); leaves divided into either 3 or 5 serrated leaflets; 5-petaled flowers white or pinkish white; dark, seedy berries.

Habitat: Evergreen and Himalayans inhabit open, uncultivated clearings; wild blackberry is more abundant in the lowland mountains.

Ah, the purple-stained hands of summer. No other wild fruit quite matches the bounty or the staining power of blackberries in the Pacific Northwest—not strawberries, salmonberries, not even huckleberries. From the lower mountain slopes of the Cascades to fields and farmland pastures, vacant lots, and the neighborhood parks of suburbia, one blackberry variety or another can be found growing wild.

Although the species hybridize freely, the Northwest boasts three basic species of blackberries. Pacific or trailing blackberries (sometimes called dewberries) are the only native species, and are most likely to be found on lower mountain slopes and in open forests and clearings. This species has long, slender, rambling vines and fine thorns. It is one of the parent plants from which loganberries, boysenberries, and some other cultivated varieties were developed.

Pacific blackberries, unlike the non-native varieties, have male and female flowers, which grow on separate plants. The five-petaled flowers of both sexes are white, but the males are larger than the females. In a male flower, the pistil (female organ) is usually stunted; in the female flower, the stamens (male organs) are underdeveloped. A bee or other pollinator acts as matchmaker. After pollination, only the female plants will bear fruit.

Their berries are neither as large nor as sweet as those of the other varieties, but many Northwesterners prefer them.

The two common invaders are Himalayan and evergreen blackberry, both of which tend to stretch and sprawl in nearly any open, uncultivated clearing. Both varieties have white to pinkish-white bisexual flowers. They are often found growing together, but the Himalayan berries are generally preferred because they are larger and sweeter. Although both have five serrated leaflets to each stem, they can be readily identified by the differences in their leaves. Evergreen leaves are narrower and much more deeply divided, and both the top and underside of the leaves are green. Himalayan leaves are noticeably wider and are green on top and whitish on the underside. The thorns of both varieties are larger, stouter, and generally more pokey than those of the Pacific blackberry.

The non-natives are aggressive and tend to form impenetrable tangles—especially the Himalayan. Its stout canes can arch about ten feet high, and root enthusiastically on contact with the ground. Blackberries found along a suburban road or field tend to be Himalayans. Each cane lives only two years. During its first year, it produces leaves but no flowers. In its second

Pacific

Evergreen

year, branches grow from the cane and produce the flowers that become juicy fruit. The cane will die afterward, but the plant's roots send up new canes following season. Birds and other animals also help to spread the seeds in their droppings. More than one hundred species of animals, including deer, chipmunks, and many birds, enjoy the bounty of blackberries.

Technically, blackberries are not berries. Those hard little seeds that get stuck between your teeth prove that these fruits are drupes, like cherries or plums. A drupe is a fleshy fruit embedded with a seed that has a hard, protective coating. Each blackberry is a cluster of small, soft drupes. After a flower is fertilized, the petals fall off and a miniature green drupe begins to form in its center.

Blackberries were first mentioned as a useful herb by the Greek physician Hippocrates, and blackberry vines and roots are still used today in some medicines. Their leaves have long been used in tea. The fruits are an excellent source of vitamin C and also contain vitamin A, calcium, potassium, and small amounts of other vitamins and minerals. What better way to get your vitamins than by sauntering out to a nearby (herbicide-free!) briar patch and filling your bucket and belly with plump, juicy blackberries?

Himalayan

Rhododendrons

Latin name: *Rhododendron* spp.

Description: Size varies considerably depending on species; fused petals form a bell shape; species offer a wide range of flower color and hues; leaves are generally thick and leathery, dark to light green.

Habitat: Acidic, well-drained soils; usually not in full sun.

You don't want to get rhododendron aficionados started talking about the attributes of their favorite flowering bush. A few hours later, you'll be wondering how you managed to overlook the wonders of the "rhody" all these years. And before you're able to quietly sneak away, true believers may even try to indoctrinate you into their cult.

Perhaps I exaggerate . . . but not by that much. There are entire books, web sites, and organizations devoted to rhodies, some of which dain to include their smaller relatives, the azaleas. In writing about rhodies, some authors have referred to "rhododendron bliss" or admitted "My affection for rhododendrons is surpassed only by love for my family." It may be impossible to understate the lure of rhododendrons.

Part of their charisma is surely due to their cheerful beauty. Most garden varieties feature big blustery clusters of blossoms in an astonishing range of colors and color combinations. There are tree species that stretch to eighty feet and dwarfs barely two inches tall. There are literally thousands of varieties of rhododendrons, often with imaginative names like Captain Jack, ice cube, cotton candy, unknown warrior, old copper, honeymoon, gypsy king, lavender girl, moonstone, jingle bells, pink petticoats, purple lace, and scintillation.

These hybrids are created by the deliberate attempts to create new varieties. But the original stock of rhodies were the wild ones, most of which came from Asia, especially from the Himalayan region's lower mountains and foothills.

The Pacific Northwest is one of the best places in North America to grow rhodies. Gardeners in many other parts of the country must coddle their precious plants, coaxing them to grow. By contrast, many Northwesteners are able to get away with just admiring the flowers of their landscape rhodies, perhaps pinching off the spent blooms, and otherwise not paying them much heed.

The Northwest is so perfectly suited for this plant that rhodies grow here in the wild. The best known of these is the Pacific rhododendron *(R. macrophyllum)* whose pink blossoms are so lovely many people include it in their yards, especially those who prefer to landscape with native plants. Visitors to the Cascades, Olympics, and the coast are often greeted by this plant in late spring or early summer. Hikers who reach timberline might also admire the less-showy white rhododendron or Cascades azalea *(R. albiflorum)*.

The natives propagate the old fashioned way, relying on bees and other insects instead of horticulturists. The bee enters the throat of the flower, drawn by the nectar inside. As it brushes past the rhodie's prominent and strategically located stamens (male organs), the bee's fuzzy coat collects pollen from it. This is inadvertently distributed to the female pistil of other flowers as the insect continues to gather foodstuff.

The natives of the Northwest are part of an extensive family that has many admirers. If you're intrigued by rhodies, a number of books and web sites offer lurid descriptions of the blossoms and leaves of umpteen varieties as well as prose as purple as some of the hybrid blooms themselves. You might also consider a trip to admire the collection at the Crystal Springs Rhododendron Garden in Portland, Oregon, or the Rhododendron Species Foundation Garden located on Weyerhaeuser's corporate campus in Federal Way, Washington—or take a walk on the wild side and visit the lovely locals.

Goldenrod

Latin name: *Solidago canadensis*

Description: To 5 feet tall; small, bright yellow flower heads clustered at top of plant form a sort of pyramid; many leaves, up to 6 inches in length, crowded on stem.

Habitat: Meadows, fields, roadsides, woodland openings, disturbed areas, fencerows.

For many years, goldenrod was unjustly accused of causing hay fever, simply because it was the most likely suspect in the vicinity. Allergy sufferers, casting about for something to blame for their late-season miseries, noted the flamboyant yellow flowers and naturally assumed the culprit had been found. In fact, it was scraggly ragweed, quietly blooming in the same area, that caused most of the itchy eyes and sneezing.

The reason why one plant annoys us and another doesn't is the difference in their pollen-dispersal techniques. Goldenrod, with its relatively heavy, sticky pollen, relies on insects accepting its loud invitation to come on over for a good time—thus its masses of showy flowers. By contrast, ragweed flowers are small, greenish, and easily overlooked. Ragweed has a different strategy: its male flowers launch a staggering number of minute pollen particles, ensuring by sheer number that some will land on waiting female flowers and fertilize them. The pollen, studded with microscopic hooks and barbs, latches onto whatever it lands on, be that female ragweed flower or human bronchial tissue.

Goldenrod has another reproductive strategy that ragweed lacks: it spreads via underground root stalks so that one plant can raise many offshoots around itself. These can form dense clusters that look more like a shrub than like several individual plants. Each plant puts forth hundreds of little gloriously-yellow flower heads, conveniently lined up for the ease of a busy pollinator. Butterflies, bumblebees, honeybees, and some beetles help spread male pollen to female pistils in their pursuit of their own foodstuff. After pollination, fuzzy little seed heads replace the flowers, and because these often stay on the plant for months, they are good fare for winter birds.

People, too, have long found uses for goldenrod. The Romans reportedly used it to help heal cuts. Its leaves have been brewed as a tonic, and during the American Revolution, they were also used in place of highly taxed English tea. People once boiled goldenrod flowers to make a yellow dye, and also chewed them for sore throats (which begs the question of whether the sick person's mouth and throat glowed golden like the flowers—but it's not advisable to find out, since the blossoms can support a poisonous fungus). And ever since Thomas Edison discovered that certain species of goldenrod contain small quantities of rubber, some have wondered whether it might be economically feasible to raise goldenrod for latex.

Perhaps goldenrod's most appreciated contribution is its beauty—especially since it blooms when so many other wildflowers have already gone to seed. As the days grow cooler and shorter, goldenrod offers one last sunny hurrah. As this plant increasingly sheds its unfair bad reputation, more and more people are adding it to their gardens and enjoying fall's sunshiny rods of gold. And that's nothing to sneeze at.

Lawn

Latin names: *Poa pratensis* (Kentucky bluegrass); *Festuca arundinacea* (tall fescue); *Lolium perenne* (perennial rye)

Description: Leaf blades form at joints along upright stem; various shades of green, depending on species and health; stems can grow several feet high unless regularly cut.

Habitat: All three of the above species grow best in full sun but can tolerate shade.

If someone tried to sell you three million tiny plants that demanded a considerable amount of maintenance, including weekly pruning throughout their growing season, you'd probably decline the offer. But most of us have (more or less willingly) planted, mowed, watered, fertilized, and weeded a lawn. For over a hundred years, cultivated grass has been an important part of American suburban living.

There are differing thoughts on how this came to be. Some sociologists have suggested that humans have a genetic predisposition to favor a savanna-like landscape; others point to peer pressure or to a desire to subdue nature. Lawns can be considered status symbols, a large open swath of grass being unattainable by the average city dweller. Or perhaps our nationwide desire for lawns has its roots in the expansive greens surrounding eighteenth-century English mansions. Both Thomas Jefferson and George Washington emulated the style on their plantations (though, needless to say, neither aristocrat wielded the scythes that kept their lawns nicely trimmed).

By 1870, an early landscape architect named Frank J. Scott had impressed upon Americans that "a smooth, closely shaven surface of grass is by far the most essential element of beauty on the grounds of a suburban home."

We've been following his advice from *The Art of Beautifying Suburban Home Grounds* ever since. Lawn care has changed from the days when Scott wrote about the bucolic joys of mowing "while the dew spangles the grass." Among many other offerings from the immense lawn care industry are a wide variety of grasses to fit America's differing climates and habitats.

The three species used most often in Pacific Northwest lawns are Kentucky bluegrass, tall fescue, and perennial rye grass, which are usually mixed together. What all kinds of grasses (wild or cultivated) have in common is a way of growing that differs from that of other plants. Consider any other type of plant—say, a tree. Its most actively growing parts are the tips of its branches; if you systematically lop these off year after year, the tree will eventually die. But because grass grows from its base, at or near the ground, we can (and indeed have to) mow it repeatedly throughout its growing season.

If grass is cut too severely (that is, if more than one-third of the total length is taken off the top), the plant becomes stressed; it responds by putting its energy into growing faster so that it can photosynthesize enough food. The optimal height to ensure the health of our most common grasses is about two inches. At this height, the grass is able to shade out tiny buds of developing weed plants, and the blades grow more slowly, while the plant puts its energy into sending its roots deeper—which results in less of a need to water.

Apparently enamored of the look of golf-course putting greens (which require a special high-maintenance grass species), most Americans cut their lawns too short for optimum health. As a result of this, and many other woes—including soil compaction, overwatering, and inappropriate use of fertilizers and insecticides—many of us who tend lawns spend an awful lot of time damaging the grass rather than helping it to grow.

Libraries and bookstores offer a number of books on how to properly care for a lawn. (Be wary, however, of any books published by chemical or professional lawn care companies, which have certain products they would like you to buy.) Healthy lawns require much less maintenance than the average American has been led to believe. But while you're looking over books, you might also consider those that discuss groundcovers and native plants as low-maintenance or no-maintenance alternatives to grass. These require not only less attention but also less water and fewer chemicals, and they don't demand a noisy, gas-guzzling, exhaust-producing lawn mower to run over them every week or so. Groundcovers and natives may ultimately prove to be the plants of the ideal suburban yard.

Queen Anne's Lace

Latin name: *Daucus carota*

Description: To 5 feet high; flat, disk-shaped, lacy white flower, 3 to 6 inches across, composed of many small clusters of flowers; one single purple floweret in center; bristly stems; fernlike leaves.

Habitat: Roadsides, fields, pastures, meadows.

Queen Anne ruled Great Britain from 1702 to 1714, but the flower named for her continues to reign over the fields, meadows, and roadsides of America. This lacy wildflower probably came to the United States by way of England, as did the childhood legend that explains its appearance: the Queen was making lace and pricked her finger, and the dark red or purple floweret in the center of the flower resulted from a spot of her blood.

But common plants often have more than one name, and this one is also known as Devil's plague (perhaps because of its tendency to take over cultivated farm fields), bird's nest (because of the way the flower, once pollinated, closes up on itself to encase the developing seeds), and wild carrot. Queen Anne's lace is indeed the wild ancestor of our familiar garden carrots. If you pull up one of the weeds, you'll see that its taproot is a pale version of a carrot. These are edible when young, but become bitter and woody as the plant grows. Trying a bite is not recommended anyway because this plant has some deadly look-alike relatives—notably poison hemlock (which killed Socrates). So, instead of taste-testing the root, crush one of the plant's fernlike leaves: you'll smell a familiar sweet aroma that reveals the carrot connection.

The plant has had many different uses over the years. The root was reportedly used by settlers as an antidote for rattlesnake bite and was also grated and applied to burns. Seeds of wild carrot were used as a contraceptive for at least twenty-five hundred years. It was once believed that eating the dark center flower would cure epilepsy. And in Queen Elizabeth's day, the ferny leaves decorated the hair of fashionable ladies on special occasions.

Queen Anne's lace blooms from May to October. Its flowers are white or, appropriately, yellowed like old lace. Each "flower" is actually made up of many little five-petaled individual flowers, with the smallest ones near the center. In each of the flowers around the edge, the outermost petal grows larger than the other four, giving the entire flower head its pleasing, symmetrical disk shape.

The individual flowers are arranged in clusters that spiral in toward the center of the plant. Neatly matching this pattern, bees land at the edge of inflorescences and work their way through the flowers by spiraling inward, gathering pollen as they go. I like to imagine that the dark central flower is a marker to inform the bee she's reached the center and must begin working in the other direction, but that is pure fantasy. The purpose of the single purple flower, if any, is a mystery.

The shallow flowers are so wide open that they would seem to run the risk of having their pollen washed right out in a summer shower. But the plant has an ingenious way around this. In wet weather, a portion of the stem about an inch or two below the flower head becomes so flexible that it no longer supports the weight of the inflorescence, and when the head bends over, the flowers are protected from the rain. (Older plants that have already lost their pollen stand tall during the most miserable storms.) The tendency of Queen Anne's lace to bow to rainstorms always reminds me that there's a lot more going on in nature than most of us realize—even among the weeds.

English Ivy

Latin name: *Hedera helix*

Description: Creeping and climbing vine; three- to five-lobed green leaves on lower plant, about 3 inches across; also nonlobed, rounded leaves almost 3 inches across; purple-black berries.

Habitat: Gardens, backyard borders, median strips, embankments, streambanks, disturbed areas, vertical structures including fences, walls, and trees.

English ivy should be sold with a warning label. Despite the refined reputation it has gained by association with prestigious colleges and quaint country cottages, English ivy becomes difficult to control when planted in the Pacific Northwest. This foreign import is liable to escape into the forest, where it runs amuck, overwhelming native plant species and holding trees hostage.

Despite its common name, English ivy is not originally from England (where it also causes damage and where its presence is increasingly controversial). The ivy's native ecosystem is the Caucasus Mountains of southern Russia, where it is kept in check by the harsh climate. In the moist, moderate climates of England and the Pacific Northwest, it grows without restraint. English ivy keeps creeping along, covering the ground and stretching up trees to eventually drape its glossy green leaves over an entire landscape.

Although ivy might appear to be a parasite that sucks the nutrients and eventually the life out of trees and other vegetation, this is not the case. Like any green plant, it is able to photosynthesize and produce its own food. But as the swelling legions of ivy-haters know, the plant's real offense is that by covering the ground it denies room to less aggressive native plants, and by climbing into trees it can become a heavy burden, one that can topple trees in a windstorm or kill off weak or diseased trees. English ivy has also been implicated in contributing to erosion and landslides during the rainy season because its shallow root system cannot hold the soil.

In an attempt to free the forests, hundreds of volunteers in various Pacific Northwest communities are participating in ivy pulls, ripping the plants from the ground by the fistfuls and slicing through the thick stems adhering to tree trunks. Cut off from its water supply, the climbing, airborne ivy cannot survive and will eventually wither and die. But just as surely as the volunteers manage to clear a few acres of the green menace, uninformed gardeners and homeowners are buying flats of fresh young ivy and planting them as a pretty, fast-growing groundcover.

Once planted, ivy begins to sprawl, sending down roots as it grows. Happening upon a vertical substrate, be it fence, building, or tree, the stem produces small white rootlets with slightly thickened tips. These tips are able to adhere to crevices and crannies, and once established, become brown, woody, and quite difficult to remove. While on the ground, and in its early climbing stages, English ivy wears its classic three- to five-lobed leaves. As it grows upright and reaches light, the leaves lose this juvenile characteristic. In a phenomenon known as dimorphism, the new leaves have a different shape: the adult leaves look rounded, as if their lobes have filled in. Eventually the adult leaves may cover the entire plant, which also becomes increasingly shrubby and dense. Once ivy reaches this mature, airborne stage it is said to be arborescent (meaning "treelike") in its growth and appearance. It may take years to reach this stage, and ivy can achieve it even without anything vertical to climb, simply by raising itself into bushy stalks.

An arborescent English ivy produces upright clusters of small greenish white flowers that, after pollination, develop into purplish black fruit. A few Northwest native birds are known to eat the berries, but they are toxic to many others. Non-natives (including the notorious English sparrow that kills Northwest native birds on their nests) eat the berries and can likely spread it via their droppings to new areas.

Many lovely, low-maintenance native plants are now available that could solve the problems created by this domineering, non-native, all-too-popular groundcover, and homeowners who like ivy should keep it under control. The plants must be regularly trimmed (and especially prevented from producing seeds) and kept from taking over ground outside the boundaries of the yard. Like the price of freedom, the price of planting English ivy in the Pacific Northwest should be eternal vigilance.

Scotch Broom

Latin name: *Cytisus scoparius*

Description: To 9 feet; stiff, short-leafed branches rise from a central point; yellow, pealike flowers; pealike seedpods with fine white hairs.

Habitat: Fields, grasslands, highway medians, roadsides, dunes, beaches.

One warm spring day, while I was driving with my mother, she commented on the pretty yellow-flowered bushes lining the roadway. She was admiring Scotch broom! I was so used to disparaging this plant that I hadn't realized how lovely its flowers were until she pointed it out.

The people of Bainbridge Island, Washington, appreciate them too. Every year they stage a celebratory Scotch broom parade. But there are plenty of people who, like me, dislike Scotch broom despite its cheery yellow flowers. In the Pacific Northwest it is considered a noxious weed, an aggressive non-native that inevitably chokes out local plants.

Scotch broom was originally brought to the Northwest in the 1850s as an ornamental. The tall, upright shrub was used to sweep floors in Scotland, which explains its common name. It is also native to Europe and North Africa and, as the shape of its flowers and seedpods suggest, is a member of the pea family. A profusion of golden flowers, sometimes edged with purple, red, or white, covers the brushy shrub in spring. The flowers, like those of sweet pea, offer insects a landing-pad petal, something like a stuck-out tongue. The flower is cleverly booby-trapped to ensure its own pollination: when the lower petals are depressed, usually by a bumblebee, the stamen thwacks the insect on the abdomen, depositing a load of pollen.

The bee then delivers the pollen to another flower as it continues to forage.

The seedpods that develop after pollination are light green and covered with fine white hairs. They turn black as they mature and dry, and eventually the two halves of the dry pod warp in opposite directions. The seeds explode from the pod with a surprisingly loud *pop!*

Scotch broom is difficult to eradicate because the plants produce so many seeds, each with a hard protective shell and capable of remaining viable for eighty years. The plant can also resprout from broken stems and must be pulled out by the roots to be defeated. This can be difficult with large specimens, however, because their water-seeking roots can burrow deep.

With the help of those long roots, Scotch broom thrives in relatively dry areas such as road cuts, hillsides, open fields, and grasslands. Bacteria on the roots are also able to "fix" nitrogen in nutrient-poor soil, meaning that the plant is able to take in nitrogen from the air and alter it so it becomes usable in the soil. For these reasons, Scotch broom was planted in the 1930s and '40s along the northern Oregon coast to stabilize drifting dunes, and it has been used elsewhere to prevent erosion. The plant is so successful, however, that it shades or crowds out less-aggressive native grasses and other plants. It can form dense brush fields standing six to nine feet tall that choke out the forage plants wild animals depend on.

But, as my mother showed me that spring day, there can be more than one way to look at Scotch broom. Some people believe that attempts to eradicate the plant are doomed. It's here and it's staying, so get used to it, they advise. When it comes to Scotch broom, you can choose to dig the plants up, or you can accept that they've found a home here—and throw a parade.

Pacific Dogwood

Latin name: *Cornus nuttallii*

Description: Can grow up to 80 feet in the open; bark thin, brown,
usually smooth; 3- to 5-inch leaves with parallel veins convening at pointed tips;
tiny greenish flowers in tight cluster surrounded by 1- to 2½-inch creamy
white leaves that look like petals; small, red, oval fruits.

Habitat: Moist soils, lower elevations.

When botanist Thomas Nuttall arrived at Fort Vancouver, at the mouth of the Columbia River, in September 1834, he hurried into the surrounding forest to study the vegetation of the "Far West." Finding some green-leaved, smooth-barked trees with clusters of red berries, he at first mistook the plant for a new species of magnolia. But after examining the next year's flower buds already poised on the branches, he recognized a family resemblance to the familiar Eastern tree called dogwood.

When those blooms erupted the following May, Nuttall noted both differences and similarities between the Eastern version and the Northwest regional tree, now called Pacific dogwood. Both trees have clusters of tiny flowers surrounded by showy white modified leaves that resemble petals. (These specialized leaves, called bracts, fill part of the job description usually reserved for flowers. The bracts invite bees and other insects to stop in for a bite to eat—all the nectar they can gather for the price of a little pollination.) The bracts of Eastern flowering dogwood are white, often tinged with green, and the outside edge of each has a single indent at the center, as if an irate insect customer had taken a bite out of them. Our Pacific dogwood has white bracts, often tinged with pink, and their tips are pointed rather than indented.

The tiny flowers, once pollinated, become clusters of brilliant red fruit. These attract a different sort of hungry customer. Birds, especially band-tailed pigeons, gobble up the fruit free of charge. The dogwood gets its payback later when the birds disperse the seeds far and wide.

The tree sometimes also enjoys a brief fall bloom. And next spring's flowers get a head start by beginning to form in the fall. These characteristic buds, which helped Nuttall recognize the Western tree, sit tight on the bare branches all winter.

Northwest tribes had specific uses for the dogwood. The Skagit dried the wood to made strong salmon spears, and other tribes used it to make game pieces for gambling. Some used the boiled bark as a tonic, a remedy that was also used by early explorers to treat malaria.

In May of 1836, Dr. John K. Townsend, a member of the expedition that included Nuttall, was called upon to treat two Cowlitz Indian children who were sick with fever. Unfortunately, he was out of quinine. He described in his journal, later published as *Narrative of a Journey Across the Rocky Mountains to the Columbia River*, how he substituted the bark of dogwood for the drug.

> Taking one of the parents into the wood with his blanket, I soon
> chipped off a plentiful supply, returned, boiled it in his own kettle,
> and completed the preparation in his lodge, with most of the

Indians standing by and staring at me to comprehend the process. This was exactly what I wished, and as I proceeded, I took some pains to explain the whole matter to them in order that they might at a future time be enabled to make use of a really valuable medicine which grows abundantly every where throughout the country. I have often thought it strange that the sagacity of the Indians should not long ago have made them acquainted with this remedy. And I believe, if they had used it, they would not have had to mourn the loss of hundreds, or even thousands of their people who have been swept away by the demon of ague and fever.

Townsend gave the children a daily dose of the extract and reported that "the second day they escaped the paroxysm, and on the third were entirely well."

In light of the sad history between the native population and the Europeans who were soon to overrun them, Pacific dogwood trees stand as an example of decency and kindness.

foxglove

Latin name: *Digitalis purpurea*

Description: Up to 6 feet; tubular flowers arranged along one side of stalk; 1½- to 2½-inch-long flowers white or rosy-purple, spots inside often dark purple ringed with white; large hairy leaves on stem.

Habitat: Gardens, roadsides, fields, forest edges.

When my friend Jenni was a ranger at Mount Rainier National Park, she was asked to pull out a big patch of foxglove. Her supervisor wanted to eradicate the plant from the park because it is not native to the Northwest. Jenni said the oddest part of the job at first was the looks she got from the tourists, taken aback by the sight of a ranger attacking the pretty flowers. But after she had worked at her task for a little while, what became odd was the way her heart was pounding. She had to stop working and sit down. Jenni later learned that digitalis, a heart stimulant, comes from foxglove; she had absorbed it through the skin of her hands.

Over two hundred years ago, physician William Withering also learned about the heart-thumping impact of foxglove—through an old woman healer in Shropshire, England. The woman brewed an herbal tea that was said to cure "the dropsy." Older people tended to suffer from dropsy (swollen feet and ankles), so named because the body's fluids seemed to drop down into the legs. When he analyzed the woman's concoction, Dr. Withering recognized that out of the twenty herbs it included, foxglove had to be the active ingredient.

Digitalis slows the heart rate, allowing the chambers more time to fill with blood, while strengthening its beats so that the weak heart accomplishes more with each contraction. This property cured the dropsy (which is caused by weakened pumping of the heart) and is also effective in treating heart failure; digitalis remains the most effective heart drug ever discovered.

The varied folklore surrounding how foxglove got its name is as interesting as the plant's medical history. On the musical end of things, a *foxesglew* or *-gleow* is an ancient instrument composed of bells hung from an arching frame. The plant's flowers may have reminded people of the bells, or the flowers used to garland the instrument during festivals may have eventually taken their name from the instrument.

And there are plenty of stories to choose from that have to do with "wee folks," or fairies. Most of these suggest that "fox" is a corruption of "folk," who used the blossoms as gloves (the spots inside the flowers marking where they had laid their fingers), or who would be offended if the foxglove were picked (this may have been meant to keep children from picking the poisonous plant). But my favorite explanation for the name is that fairies gave the flowers to foxes to wear like gloves on their dainty feet so they could sneak into chicken coops and quietly raid them.

Foxglove is a biennial, which means that it spends its first year making leaves and storing energy in its root, and produces blossoms in its second year. Its fused petals look like purple tubes (although cultivated garden varieties now come in many delightful colors) and open successively from the bottom upward. Foxglove blooms from May through September, and its inviting flowers attract hummingbirds and bees. The pollinated flowers then become seeds from which new plants will bloom after two years' time—unless a (gloved) ranger on a mission gets to them first.

Maples

Latin names: *Acer macrophyllum* (bigleaf maple); *A. circinatum* (vine maple)

Description: Lobed leaves, dark green above and paler green below, turning color in autumn; twin seeds each have veined wings; bark is gray when tree is young, turning reddish brown as it ages.

Habitat: Moist soils.

The first time I sat at my sister-in-law Treesa's dinner table, I paid more attention to its wood grain than to the meal she served on it. Instead of the straight lines or elongated loops of most wood, this table's grain drew scribbles. Against their lighter background, the dark brown meandering curves looked like the outlines of puffy cumulus clouds. This wood, Treesa explained, was called "curly maple." Curly maple is found near the base of some specimens of bigleaf maple, and its curious grain is prized by furniture makers. (Big, abnormal bulges called burls are also sometimes

found, and these are used to create decorative pieces.)

Because maples typically grow near creeks and scattered among other species, they not as easy to harvest as other trees—nor is their wood strong enough for structural use—so they are not a large part of the Northwest lumber market. They are, however, a large part of our forests—especially the ubiquitous vine maple. This tree and its close relative the bigleaf maple are two of the most obvious broadleaf trees in a land of conifers. Both are native.

If there were a prize for largest leaves among all the maple species, bigleaf would win it. This tree could also claim the title of the only large maple growing naturally in the Western states. Bigleaf can grow as high as eighty feet, its reddish brown bark becoming ridged as it ages and often sporting patches of moss. In spring, small yellow flowers dangle from the naked branches in four- to six-inch-long clusters. Then the monster five-lobed leaves unfurl, eventually spreading as wide as twelve inches and almost equally long. These turn a warm, rich yellow in the fall before dropping to rest on the forest floor.

But if there were a prize for prettiest autumn color among native trees, vine maple would easily beat bigleaf: its foliage bursts into a raucous red. Vine maple's biggest leaves are only half the size of its relation's and might be considered chubby by comparison. If you were to trace around a leaf's margins, without dipping down into the shallow V's made by its seven or nine lobes, you would transcribe a nearly perfect circle.

It should be mentioned that vine maple would also probably win a contest for vegetation most likely to trip an unsuspecting hiker. When it grows in deep forests, it tends to send long, slender, vinelike limbs snaking across the forest floor in search of sunlight. The French voyageurs who had to portage their canoes through its tangled sprawl called it "devil wood." Vine maple sends up many upright slender trunks, but usually grows no higher than thirty feet. Straddling the line between tree and bush, it may be classified as either, depending on the shape it assumes as it grows.

Vine maple's small white flowers hang in loose clusters in spring. Both bigleaf and vine maple produce male and female flowers in the same cluster. After fertilization by bees and other insects, the female flowers develop into the familiar winged maple seeds. These are eaten by squirrels, chipmunks, mice, woodrats, finches, and grosbeaks, which help to disperse the seeds throughout the forest.

Bigleaf is also called Oregon maple, and vine maple is sometimes called mountain maple. Their genus name, *Acer,* refers to the maple family; bigleaf's species name *macrophyllum* translates neatly to "big leaf," and vine maple's *circinatum* means "round," which describes the circular outline of the leaves. Plenty of plants, regardless of how fitting their Latin names might be, have ended up saddled with obscure, ill-fitting common names. But both these maples are well served by their descriptive names of bigleaf and vine.

Red Alder

Latin name: *Alnus rubra*

Description: To over 100 feet; bark mottled white or gray; oval, saw-toothed leaves, about 2 to 6 inches long, green above and light below.

Habitat: Moist or wet open areas, including streamsides, wetlands, mudflow deposits, clearcut and burned areas.

When you work as a naturalist, you learn not to laugh when visitors ask you questions like "What time does your three o'clock talk start?" and "Is the cave underground?" or even "When do the deer turn into elk?" So when a woman stopped me to ask, "What's the name of the tree that has both leaves and pine cones?" I carefully considered her question. While no broadleaf tree has true cones, the alder certainly *looks* like it does.

The reproductive parts of alder are their male and female catkins, and it is the fertilized female catkins that resemble miniature conifer cones. Male catkins, four to six inches long, hang tassel-like under the branches, while the smaller female buds grow on top of the branches. After fertilization, the female catkin develops into a small woody cone one-half to one inch high. Tucked inside its small scales are tiny seeds, which are dispersed by the wind. Because the durable female catkins hang on long after the leaves have fallen, alder can be readily identified by its cones even during the bare-branch days of winter.

And, viewed from a distance, the rosy cast of red alders is one of the first signs to winter-rain-weary Northwesterners that spring is finally on its way. The "red" of red alders, however, probably refers to the inner wood of the tree. Beneath that white or gray lichen-covered exterior is a red tree. Native Americans used the inner bark to make a reddish dye that, when applied to nets, made them virtually invisible to fish. The rest of the tree had many different uses. The leaves and bark have astringent properties and were applied to wounds to curb bleeding. The bark, steeped into a tea, was used to treat rheumatic fever (science later identified salicin in the bark as the curative agent; it continues to be used in modern medicine). Because the wood is tasteless, it was perfect to use for bowls and eating utensils. And alder was—and still is—the wood of choice for smoking salmon.

Many animals also have use for red alder. Elk, deer, and mountain beaver nip off fresh twigs. Beavers and porcupines prefer the inner bark. And tent caterpillars go hog-wild over the leaves. About every ten years or so, the populations of these moth larvae explode, so that it appears every red alder in an area is loaded with the little chewing machines and their

root·nodules host beneficial bacteria

"Cones"

gauzy protective tents. The trees fight back by producing unpalatable tannin in their leaves. Even uninfested red alders mount this defense, apparently alerted to the attack by neighboring trees that announce the message in pheromones carried by the wind. In this cycle, the tent caterpillar moth population is beaten back by the combination of tree response and fat and happy predators like birds and parasites. Few alders are actually killed, though it may take them a year or two to fully recover from the onslaught.

Red alder is both the Pacific Northwest's most common broadleaf tree and its most commercially valuable one. But in a land where conifer is king, red alder was disparaged by foresters for many years. After an area was clearcut, Douglas-fir seedlings were planted, one at a time, by hoedad and hand. The sun-loving alders, meanwhile, were planted far more easily by the wind. Alder is quick to take advantage of newly open areas like those resulting from stream erosion, fire—or clearcutting. To the foresters' consternation, alder grew faster than Douglas-fir, shading the young conifers and slowing their growth. In response, foresters tried their best to eradicate alder on their plantations.

But the story of alders is the stuff of fairy tales, where the ugly duckling becomes a swan, or the frog is ultimately revealed as a prince. The happily-ever-after ending began when researchers in the Forest Service's Wind River Experimental Forest noticed that Douglas-firs interspersed with alders were larger and healthier than those growing in nearby monocultures. Unlike any other tree in the Pacific Northwest, alder is able to take nitrogen from the air and infuse it into the soil. The roots of alder (like those of legumes) host bacteria that convert the nitrogen into a form that can be taken up by other plants. The decaying, fallen leaves of alder also add nitrogen, and they break down much faster than conifer needles, adding humus to the soil. In addition, alder, like a knight in shining armor, actually protects and defends its companions. Alder roots secrete a toxin that kills the fungus that causes a root rot deadly to Douglas-firs. When this fact was recognized, humbled foresters began replanting red alder in the areas where root rot had killed Doug-firs.

The happy ending to this story is one of many that could be told about red alder. *A Broadleaf Tree Has Cones*; *The White-Barked Tree's Red Heart: Traditional Use by Animals and People*; and *Communication Among Trees* would all fit together nicely on a bookshelf made of alder wood.

Rainbows

If you know Roy G. Biv, then you know something about rainbows. "Roy G. Biv" is not a person—it's the acronym for the order in which a rainbow's colors are always arrayed: red, orange, yellow, green, blue, indigo, violet. The top color in a rainbow's arc is red, and the other colors fall in order underneath. When a second rainbow appears above the primary one (making a double rainbow), its colors are in the same order but reversed: violet is at the top of the arc, red at the bottom. The order of the colors was pointed out by Isaac Newton in 1660. (Many scientists today suggest that indigo, which is so similar to violet, should not be included in the lineup.)

The reason the colors are always arrayed the same way has something to do with how rainbows form in the first place. But to me, that explanation seems to require nearly as much faith in science as the Greeks had in the belief that the goddess of the rainbow bridged the worlds of gods and mortals. To begin with, science insists that what we perceive as white light is actually comprised of all the colors of the rainbow. Despite my acquaintance with Roy G. Biv, this has always struck me as counterintuitive. After all, if you scribbled all six crayon colors together, wouldn't the result be closer to black than white?

Even the rainbow that streams from a prism—the sight of which caused Newton to realize that each color is bent to a slightly different angle— seems to my mind more a trick of the cut glass than a revelation. If you are similarly puzzled, here's how to see the light. Draw a circle, divided evenly into six wedges. Give each wedge one of the rainbow colors—this works best if the colors are lightly applied. Spin the circle (called a Newton's disc) and—*voilà*—your eye perceives a disk of white.

Now that you're convinced that six colors weave into white, the next question is how they become untangled in a rainbow. Three things are required to see a rainbow: the observer, sunlight, and small drops of water to act as prisms to bend the light, forcing each color to emerge at its own particular angle. Raindrops can do this, of course, but water sprayed from a garden hose, fountain, waterfall, or even the crest of a wave can perform the same magic.

To see a rainbow, the observer must be positioned between the sun and the water drops. Thus, rainbows are seen in the west in the morning (as the sun rises in the east) or in the east in the afternoon (as the sun sinks in the west). We cannot see them when the sun is too high overhead. Nor can we see them unless the water drops are appropriately shaped to reflect the light. Drops that are too large become distorted by air pressure. Fine drops less than one-sixteenth of an inch in diameter, like those at the tail end of a rain shower, maintain a nearly spherical shape that is able to reflect light.

Early investigators used water-filled glass vials as stand-ins for raindrops, and visualizing these larger, spherical "drops" helps to clarify what happens when sunlight enters a raindrop. Some sunlight simply passes right through the drop, but that light which strikes at just the right angle is bent slightly and separated into its ordered colors. These colors then hit the back of the drop, which reflects them, and they are further separated as they travel out the front of the drop. Which of these fanned colors strikes your eye depends on the angle formed by that drop, the sun, and your eye.

Of course, a particular raindrop's angle to your eye changes as it falls, and therefore so does the color it reflects toward your eye: red to orange to yellow to green, etc. In other words, as you gaze at a rainbow, you are watching innumerable raindrops, each one flashing changing colors at your eye as it falls—but at any frozen moment in time you would perceive only a single color from each individual raindrop.

A double rainbow forms in the same way, except that the sunlight enters the drop at a different angle and is reflected twice before it emerges. This not only reverses the order of the colors, it also dims them because more light is lost from the ray in the transaction. The resulting secondary bow is necessarily dimmer, and its colors are in the opposite order than those of the primary bow.

Whether the colored ribbons you see are single or double, each rainbow you see can be said to be your very own. Since the angles between the sun, the raindrops, and any two people are different (no two people can occupy the same exact space), all of us perceive our own particular rainbows.

The North Star, the Big Dipper, and Orion

To get oriented while looking at the night sky, it helps to find Polaris, the North Star. And to find the North Star, it might help to find the Big Dipper, the grouping of stars most of us learned to recognize in childhood. Gazing northward, it's easy to pick out the familiar seven stars that make up the handle and bowl of the dipper. Trace an imaginary straight line through the two bowl stars farthest from the handle (called the "pointers") and follow the line to the brightest star in that region of the sky, the North Star. By happenstance, the Earth's north pole tilts toward this star, also called the Pole Star, so on a clear night we in the Northern Hemisphere can always determine true north.

Using the North Star as a starting point, and with the help of a handy star guide, we can also learn to recognize other constellations. The North Star remains relatively constant as the other stars slowly revolve around it. Despite appearances, it's not the night sky that is moving. This optical illusion is produced by the Earth's rotation, which spins us around underneath the sky in a twenty-four-hour cycle. Thus the Big Dipper may begin the night positioned as if it were emptying its bowl, but as the night progresses, it arcs around in a huge counterclockwise circle to stand on its handle before again rolling around as if to empty itself.

Because the Earth is also orbiting the sun, the Big Dipper can be found at the same time each night in a slightly different place in its circular promenade. It begins the summer nights in position to empty its bowl, but by the same hour in winter, it begins by standing on its handle. Due to that annual rotation, some constellations, such as Orion the Hunter, can be seen only for part of the year. In winter, you can find Orion in the southern sky by facing away from Polaris and the Big Dipper and looking for three bright stars in a tilting line. These easy-to-locate stars make up Orion's belt. Four bright stars making a trapezoid shape mark Orion's body, and his sword is a cluster of fainter stars pointing downward from his belt. Tracing his upraised club and protecting shield might require the help of a star guide. Binoculars or a simple telescope also help to bring into focus particulars such as the star Betelgeuse, the bright upper-left star of the trapezoid (Orion's shoulder).

Betelgeuse (pronounced "beetle-juice" or "BEH-tel-jooz") glows reddish orange through binoculars. It is a supergiant star, so called because it is much more massive than our own sun—over a thousand times larger, in fact. Rigel ("RY-jel"), located on a diagonal from Betelgeuse and marking Orion's foot, is considerably smaller (but still large enough to be classified as a giant compared to our sun). Rigel burns even brighter than Betelgeuse, however, and shines with a bluish cast. The colors of stars (including the sun's yellow) reveal their temperatures. Stars are hot balls of gas, and they show colors something like an iron poker that glows red when heated and fires up to white-hot. An estimate of the relatively cool, reddish Betelgeuse pegs it at three thousand degrees C., puts our yellowish sun's surface at six thousand degrees C., and white-hot Rigel at twenty thousand degrees C.

In addition to allowing closer observation of Betelgeuse and Rigel, binoculars will also help you view an area within Orion where astronomers believe stars are being born. The hazy area in the middle of Orion's sword is a mass of gases and dust called a nebula. The Orion Nebula is a nursery for stars.

Orion is one of the easiest constellations to find—at least during the part of the year when it can be seen. The good old Big Dipper, itself part of the constellation known as the Great Bear or Ursa Major, is more dependable. And we can always count on the stalwart North Star to point the way.

Selected References

Arno, Stephen F. *Northwest Trees.* Seattle: The Mountaineers, 1977.

Ball, Jeff, and Liz Ball. *Smart Yard: 60-Minute Lawn Care.* Golden, Colorado: Fulcrum Publishing, 1994.

Berrisford, Judith. *Rhododendrons & Azaleas.* New York: St. Martin's Press, 1964.

Corkran, Charlotte C., and Chris Thoms. *Amphibians of Oregon, Washington, and British Columbia: A Field Identification Guide.* Edmonton, Alberta: Lone Pine Publishing, 1996.

Ehrlich, Paul R., et al. *The Birder's Handbook: A Field Guide to the Natural History of North American Birds.* New York: Simon & Schuster Inc., 1988.

Fitzgerald, Terrence D. *The Tent Caterpillars.* Ithaca, New York: Cornell University Press, 1995.

Gordon, David George. *The Western Society of Malacologists Field Guide to the Slug.* Seattle: Sasquatch Books, 1994.

Gunther, Erna. *Ethnobotany of Western Washington.* Seattle and London: University of Washington Press, 1973.

Lawrence, Gale. *A Field Guide to the Familiar.* New York: Prentice Hall Press, 1987.

_____. *The Beginning Naturalist: Weekly Encounters with the Natural World.* Shelburne, Vermont: The New England Press, 1979.

Leopold, Luna B., and Kenneth S. Davis. *Water.* New York: Time Incorporated, 1966.

Maser, Chris. *Mammals of the Pacific Northwest: From the Coast to the High Cascades.* Corvallis: Oregon State University Press, 1998.

Mathews, Daniel. *Cascade-Olympic Natural History: A Trailside Reference.* Portland, Oregon: Raven Editions, 1999.

McKenny, Margaret. *Wildlife of the Pacific Northwest.* Portland, Oregon: Binfords & Mort, 1954.

Milne, Lorus, and Margery Milne. *National Audubon Society Field Guide to North American Insects and Spiders.* New York: Alfred A. Knopf, Inc., 1980.

Pasachoff, Jay M., and Donald H. Menzel. *A Field Guide to the Stars and Planets.* Boston: Houghton Mifflin Company, 1997.

Peattie, Donald Culross. *A Natural History of Western Trees.* Cambridge, Massachusetts: The Riverside Press, 1953.

Pyle, Robert Michael. *National Audubon Society Field Guide to North American Butterflies.* New York: Alfred A. Knopf, Inc., 1997.

Rose, Peter Q. *The Gardener's Guide to Growing Ivies.* Portland, Oregon: Timber Press, 1996.

Stokes, Donald W. *A Guide to Observing Insect Lives.* Boston: Little, Brown and Co., 1983.

Stokes, Donald W., and Lillian Q. Stokes. *A Guide to Animal Tracking and Behavior.* Boston: Little, Brown and Co., 1983.

_____. *A Guide to Bird Behavior, Volume III.* Boston: Little, Brown and Co., 1989.

Storm, Robert M., and William P. Leonard, eds. *Reptiles of Washington and Oregon.* Seattle: Seattle Audubon Society, 1995.

Terres, John K. *The Audubon Society Encyclopedia of North American Birds.* New York: Alfred A. Knopf, Inc., 1987.

Tufts, Craig, and Peter Loewer. *Gardening for Wildlife: How to Create a Beautiful Backyard Habitat for Birds, Butterflies, and Other Wildlife.* Emmaus, Pennsylvania: Rodale Press, Inc./Round Stone Press, 1995.

Tweedie, Michael. *Insect Life.* London: William Collins Sons & Co., 1977.

Van Veen, Ted. *Rhododendrons in America.* Portland, Oregon: Sweeney, Krist & Dimm, Inc., 1969.

Whitaker, John O., Jr. *National Audubon Society Field Guide to North American Mammals.* New York: Alfred A. Knopf, 1997.

Zajonc, Arthur. *Catching the Light: The Entwined History of Light and Mind.* New York: Oxford University Press, 1993.

Index

D

Daddy longlegs, 113
Dandelion, 142
Dark-eyed junco, 31
Daucus carota, 155
Deer mouse, 10
Deroceras reticulatum, 83
Devil's plauge, 155
Dewberries, 145
Didelphis marsupialis, 16
Digitalis purpurea, 166
Dissosteira spp., 90
Dogwood, Pacific, 163
Double rainbow, 177
Dove, mourning, 71

E

Earthworm, 107
Earwig, European, 139
Eastern cottontail rabbit, 22
Eastern gray squirrel, 7
English ivy, 158
European black slug, 83
European earwig, 139
European ground beetle, 124
European rabbit, 22
European starling, 40
Evergreen blackberry, 145

f

Falco sparverius, 51
Fall webworms, 101
Fescue, tall, 152
Festuca arundinacea, 152
Field cricket, 137
Flickers, 48
Fly, crane, 135

Forficula auricularia, 139
Formica obscuripes, 93
Foxglove, 166
Frog, Pacific chorus, 20
Frog, Pacific treefrog, 19
Froghopper, 119

G

Garden slugs, 83
Geese, Canada, 74
Goldenrod, 150
Goldfinch, American, 60
Grass, 152
Grasshoppers, 90
Gray garden slug, 83
Great Bear, 179
Great gray garden slug, 83
Ground beetles, 124
Gryllus assimilis, 137

H–J

Harvestmen, 115
Hawk
    red-tailed, 77
    sharp-shinned, 34
    sparrow, 51
Hedera helix, 158
Himalayan blackberry, 145
Hirundo spp., 57
Hummingbird, rufous, 28
Hyla regilla, 19
Hyphantria cunea, 101
Isabella tiger moth, 105
Isia isabella, 105
Ivy, English, 158
Junco hyemalis, 31
Juncos, 31

K-L

Kentucky bluegrass, 152
Kestrel, American, 51
Killdeer, 45
Ladybird beetle, 96
Ladybugs, 96
Lawn, 152
Limax maximus, 83
Locusts, 90
Lolium perenne, 152
Long-horned grasshopper, 91
Longlegs, daddy, 113
Long-winged locust, 90
Lumbricus terrestris, 107

M

Malacosoma californicum, 99
Mantis religiosa, 86
Mantis, praying, 86
Maples, 168
Meadow spittlebug, 119
Melospiza melodia, 62
Mephitis mephitis, 25
Milky slug, 83
Mole, Townsend's, 13
Mosquito, 126
Mosquito eater, 135
Moth
    Isabella tiger, 105
    western tent caterpillar, 99
Mountain maple, 170
Mourning cloak butterfly, 110
Mourning dove, 71
Mouse, deer, 10

N-O

North Star, 178
Northern flicker, 48
Northwestern crow, 66
Northwestern garter snake, 80
Nymphalis antiopa, 110
Oniscus asellus, 132
Opossum, 16
Oregon junco, 33
Oregon maple, 170
Oregon towhee, 43
Orion, 178
Oryctolagus cuniculus, 22

P

Pacific blackberry, 145
Pacific chorus frog, 20
Pacific dogwood, 163
Pacific rhododendron, 149
Pacific treefrog, 19
Parasite bumblebees, 129
Parus atricapillus, 1
Passenger pigeon, 72
Perennial rye, 152
Peromyscus maniculatus, 10
Petrochelidon pyrrhonota, 57
Phalangium opilio 115
Phasianus colchicus, 54
Pheasant, ring-necked, 54
Philaenus spumarius, 119
Pigeon, passenger, 72
Pillbugs, 132
Pipilo spp., 42
Plant lice, 104
Poa pratensis, 152
Polaris, 178
Pole Star, 178
Porcellio scaber, 132

U-Z

Wanna Get Really Wild?

MORE Uncommon field Guides

by Patricia K. Lichen
Illustrations by Linda M. Feltner

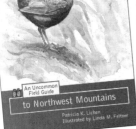

Mountains

River-Walking Songbirds & Singing Coyotes
An Uncommon Field Guide to Northwest Mountains

Marmots sharing sentinel duty. Songbirds walking underwater.
Hidden relationships between chanterelle mushrooms and Douglas-
fir trees. Discover the marvels and mating habits, behaviors and
best-kept secrets of a host of plants, birds, animals, and natural
phenomenon of Northwest mountains.

Coast & Wetlands

Brittle Stars & Mudbugs
An Uncommon Field Guide to
Northwest Shorelines & Wetlands

Body-surfing otters. Racing razor clams. Water-striding insects.
Edible cattails. Let this *Uncommon Field Guide* escort you
along the fascinating beaches, rocky shorelines, estuaries,
rivers, and marshlands of the Pacific Northwest.

SASQUATCH BOOKS
SEATTLE

Available at fine stores everywhere
Call toll-free 800-775-0817 to order or visit www.SasquatchBooks.com

Alistair
Frank

Pierre Herman

Nathalie Haas